LAST POEMS

Vincent Buckley was born in 1925 in Romsey, Victoria. He was educated at St Patrick's College, Melbourne, joined the RAAF during the war, was invalided out, and went to Melbourne University, where he majored in Philosophy, Economics, and English, and was active in the ALP Club. He married and had two daughters. While tutoring in English, he produced *Essays in Poetry: Mainly Australian*; and in Cambridge on the Mannix scholarship he wrote *Poetry and Morality*.

Back in Melbourne, he co-founded the magazine *Prospect*, and later became poetry editor for the *Bulletin*. From 1967 he held a personal chair in Poetry at Melbourne University, and produced *Poetry and the Sacred*.

In 1969 he founded the Committee for Civil Rights in Ireland, and throughout his life he visited and lived in Ireland often. He married again and had two more daughters. He loved horse-racing, music and painting. He published two books of cultural analysis in autobiographical mode, *Cutting Green Hay* and *Memory Ireland*, and retired early to write more cultural history as well as poetry.

He edited the *Faber Book of Modern Australian Verse*. His many prizes for poetry included the Christopher Brennan award, and his books include *The World's Flesh*, *Masters in Israel*, *Arcady and Other Places*, *Golden Builders*, *The Pattern*, *Late-Winter Child* and *Selected Poems*.

He died in 1988.

VINCENT BUCKLEY

Last poems

McPHEE GRIBBLE

McPhee Gribble
Penguin Books Australia Ltd
487 Maroondah Highway, P.O. Box 257
Ringwood, Victoria 3134
Penguin Books Ltd
Harmondsworth, Middlesex, England
Viking Penguin, A Division of Penguin Books USA Inc.
375 Hudson Street, New York, New York 10014, USA
Penguin Books Canada Limited
10 Alcorn Avenue, Toronto, Ontario, Canada M4V 1E4
Penguin Books (N.Z.) Ltd
182–190 Wairau Road, Auckland 10, New Zealand

First published by Penguin Books Australia Ltd 1991
This revised edition published by Penguin Books Australia Ltd 1991

10 9 8 7 6 5 4 3 2 1

Copyright © Penelope Buckley, 1991

All rights reserved. Without limiting the rights under copyright reserved above, no part of this publication may be reproduced, stored in or introduced into a retrieval system, or transmitted, in any form or by any means (electrical, mechanical, photocopying, recording or otherwise) without the prior written permission of both the copyright owner and the above publisher of this book.

Produced by McPhee Gribble
487 Maroondah Highway, Ringwood, Victoria 3134, Australia
A division of Penguin Books Australia Ltd

Designed by Meredith Parslow
Typeset in 10½/11½ Bembo by Bookset, Melbourne
Printed in Australia by Australian Print Group, Melbourne

Frontispiece photo of the poet in the 1980s by courtesy Penelope Buckley.

National Library of Australia
Cataloguing-in-Publication data:
Buckley, Vincent, 1925–1988.
  Last poems.

  New ed.
  ISBN 0 86914 270 4.

    I. Title.

A821.3

The good news is, it's almost finished now
Time for some poems and some poems to
         daughters   grow
For me, familiar fragments of the earth to
Remember me: I lived too hard, but touch
                                    not too much.

Unfinished poem
by Vincent Buckley

CONTENTS

Foreword by Penelope Buckley xi
Acknowledgements xiv

A Poetry Without Attitudes

Winds drain 3
The good days begin 4
Making Friends 5
Spring's Come 6
Seasons 7
A Leaf from the Firestorm 8
Pound's Grave 9
Airletter to Craig Raine 10
They come at intervals 11
Moonlight Flit (of Possums) 12
Soft War Poems 13
Kerbside 19
Wittgenstein's Face 20
The Iceland Foxes 21
Remember Mortality 22
Nothing Outside the Text 24
'The camps' 25
That is what they taught him 26
The instructor of nightmares 27
How will civilisation last? 28
Gulag I 29
Public Poetry 30
Holiness of the Meat Trade. 31
Having revised our gods 32
Scientific Scanning 33
Letter Home 34
Portnoy's Revenge 35
Said the Taxi-Driver 36
Hear how the Irish speak pentameters. . . 37
Gulag II 38
Perfect Pitch 39
Untitled Series 40
Tips for Performers 44

Teaching German Literature	45
Piccolo Spoleto	46
My Mother's Anzacs	47
Hunger-Strike	50
Digging In	57
Notes from Blackhall	59
Natura Naturans	64
The Coven	65
Louisa Stewart is Foaling	67
The Curragh in Cold Autumn	69
Sheela-na-Gig	70
The Lake	71
Triads	72
Birthday Suite for Seamus Heaney	73
Recovery Suite for Thomas Kinsella	77
Girl Memory	82
Revising	83
Looking down Thomas Street	84
The House That	85
Emigrants from Ireland	86
Showing Off for the Pipes	87
Cambs as a State of Colour	88
Small Brown Poem for Grania Buckley	89
The neighbours	90
Leaving	91
Ars medica	92
Names	93
Theories	94
The Too-Lateness	95
Narrative	98
Conversations	99
Love	100
Sheer Warmth	101
A Tincture of Budapest	102
Deathmares	104
Trumpet Voluntary	105
An Easy Death	106
Memory: the hinge	108
Down Scannell Lane	109
Waterbeach	110

Telephone, old friend	111
Booze Years	112
But wouldn't you be pleased?	114
Sydney Visit	115
Life Style	117
Getting Away	118
Hospital Summer, Western Suburbs . . .	119
Nervy city	123
I've forgotten the names	124
The Tuning-Time	125
Old Jazz Persons.	126
Brunny Town Hall	127
Three days to the loss of summer . . .	128
A man, a woman	129
Oral History	130
Introvert as Horseman	131
Seabreeze	132
We knew that the sea was heaven . . .	134
Often the plate held black trout	135
Deep of Evening	136
Brothers	138
Lights glint on dust	140
Brought up on the Fears of Women . . .	141
The Table	144
Seeing Romsey	145
The Child is Revenant to the Man . . .	146
A Poetry Without Attitudes	147

The Watch's Wheel – Pieces and Songs

A longing for what you have been reading . .	151
These in Their Wet Darkness	152
Maps	152
The South Side of Dublin	152
Castle Bees.	153
'I have tried'	154
Fine Western Land	154
The clarinet produced a clear colour . . .	156
Over and over again	157
Dreamed	158
'All my life I hated afternoons'	158

I hated summers, and weekends	159
So many years ago	160
Weird love	160
One put down his notebook	161
It is like a work rhythm	161
Night-Walker	162
Series towards a longer 'Brought up on the Fears of Women'	163
Piece towards a longer 'Brought up on the Fears of Women'	168
Introduction for a Blues	169
Two in a bed	169
We made love on a daybed	169
There, where the committee voted	170
I am leftwing going on rightwing	170
Money like lava	171
To write now	171
I was no soldier	172
Bard-Price	172
Dialogues	173
My instinct is to sing death songs	174
For A. D. Hope	175
For Brigid on Her Twentieth Birthday	176
Birthday Poem for Grania	177
Susannah's Valentine	177
Rudolph Valentino	178
Small Green Poem for Grania Buckley	178
For Susannah, on returning from the Wards	178
You were walking	179
Though I act out love	180
Birthday Poem 2	181
Hill-Road	182
Burren	183
I have you poised in the mind	183
Sea-Mammal Songs	185
Sit on the counter, girl	188
Parson Dadewell	188
I wrote a letter to Seamus	189
Child of Ardmore	190
Ardmore Bay	191

FOREWORD

When Vincent Buckley died, in November 1988, he had not published a book of poetry for seven years. He left a large body of poems on word-processor in the Melbourne University English Department, of which some had been published in periodicals in the same or earlier versions; and he also left a house deep in other poems, finished and unfinished, typed and in manuscript, some in notebooks and dated, others on cheque-butts and betting slips and envelopes. *Last Poems* includes virtually everything that was on the word-processor, together with what seemed to me (with the help of some discerning advice from Chris Wallace-Crabbe) to be the best and most finished of the rest.

The poems on word-processor were not arranged, but about half of them, according to a list of contents left in manuscript, were intended to form a separate volume called *A General Order for the Night*. Over a number of years Vincent had discussed with Hilary McPhee their joint wish that she should publish his poetry, and, when it started to seem really possible at last, he planned this collection to show her.

For reasons stemming from his death, I wanted to see the remaining poetry brought out in one volume; but I also wanted to follow his intention, and at first *A General Order for the Night* headed the present collection, as the first of three sections. When placed beside the others, however, it appeared both to Chris and to Hilary to be a little too concentrated and unrelieved for the balance of the whole, and in the light of their opinions (which I came to share) I considered other possibilities. The result is that *A General Order for the Night* has disappeared as a title; its contents and their sequence have been kept almost entire (with the displacement only of 'Hunger-Strike' and a few short poems); and it has been set inside and at two points interlaced with the second collection, whose title – *A Poetry Without Attitudes* – is now given to both.

This containment and interlacing suits the arrangement as a whole, for it aims at the contrapuntal, or at a systolic/diastolic variation to use a favourite term of Vincent's: an alternating rhythm of introversion and extraversion, concentration and dispersal. The general arrangement of the other poems was mine, but it was made on the basis of what I take to be this ground feature of his later poetry.

A Poetry Without Attitudes now contains all the poems on the word-processor and a few others which thematically belonged. The title suggested itself: it occurs, of course, in the two framing poems, and seems to me to invoke the spirit of his creative endeavour in the final years. He said something close to this in an interview with Paul Kavanagh in *Southerly* in 1987:

> I have written a poem which is called 'Poetry Without Attitudes'. It says in effect, 'Wouldn't that be great, to end your life with friends without envy, a couple of other things, and poetry without attitudes.' I may put a bit of this poem as a motto for my next book.

The Watch's Wheel, the second part of *Last Poems*, is something of a workshop collection – pieces, poems, songs – which had something to offer that ought not be lost. Many are finished poems, including some in draft. Some are occasional and some impromptu. A few are old. Most of them had never been typed. The Ardmore songs were written for the children of the Ardmore school to sing and set to music by the headmaster, Victor Mullins. 'Rudolph Valentino' was sung in the car while we were travelling; so was 'Teaching German Literature', which was later recalled and given to the word-processor. There is some serious work-in-progress, and some savagely satirical vignettes.

The internal dating in 'Dialogues' underlines the fact that he was writing finished poetry until a few days before he died.

There were many instances of unresolved alternatives – usually only for a single word, but one short poem might contain several. Generally it was clear why they were unresolved: the advantages and disadvantages were finely balanced. In these cases I made the choices *ad hoc* myself, and I have not attempted to document them here. They occur only in *The Watch's Wheel*, and since the manuscripts, or their facsimiles, are intended for the library at the Australian Defence Force Academy, anyone who is curious about these details will be able to examine them themselves.

The same applies to the variant versions of whole poems in both collections. Most were easy enough to read chronologically, but a few were not, as Vincent sometimes made parallel or at least lateral revisions.

The punctuation is not always consistent either in typescript or in manuscript – the book's editor Judith Lukin and I have intervened as little as possible.

The only poem whose editing needs any particular explanation is 'An Easy Death'. When it was first published (in *Meanjin* 2/1984) this poem ended with the lines beginning, 'Lights glint on dust', which appear separately here on page 4. These lines were separated on the word-processor, though still sequent, and I chose to interpret this as meaning that they and what went before no longer constituted a single poem. Plainly, I may be wrong. If so, I have extended the principle of counterpoint somewhat beyond what was reasonable, but I do not think the poetry suffers by it.

All the poems on word-processor were typed by Eileen Whittaker. Many in *The Watch's Wheel* were typed by Grania Buckley. Chris Wallace-Crabbe not only gave invaluable advice but single-handedly reduced *The Watch's Wheel* to just over half its projected size. Carolyn Masel helped to locate the published versions of poems. Susannah Buckley advised about some poems, and Anne Coulthurst gave much general support over several years. *The Bargeman* was suggested for the cover and also lent by Brigid Buckley. Warm gratitude is offered to them all.

It has been a great pleasure and an honour to work on Vincent's behalf with Hilary McPhee and her editor Judith Lukin and her designer Meredith Parslow. It has been all he could have wanted, and I wish he could have had that pleasure directly himself.

Vincent's own instinct, when publishing a book of poetry, was always to pare down, select, reduce. I hope he will forgive me for following a more inclusive principle towards this last rich *aetas* in his work which will not be succeeded by another.

Penelope Buckley
April 1991

ACKNOWLEDGEMENTS

Some of these poems have appeared previously in the *Age*, the *Bulletin*, *Fine Line*, *Helix*, *Mattoid*, *Meanjin*, the *New Statesman*, *Northern Perspective*, *Outrider*, *Overland*, *Poetry Ireland*, *Quarry*, *Scripsi*; and in *Australian Poetry 1988* (ed. Vivian Smith, Angus & Robertson), *Neither Nuked nor Crucified and other poems* (ed. Christopher Pollnitz, University of Newcastle, 1984), *The Tinwash Dish* (ed. John Tranter).

*A
Poetry
Without
Attitudes*

Winds drain, mosses chill
the deepest fuels of the body.
Nothing brings good or ill.
I have reached Li Po's age
and feel immortal.

That would be worth it:
friend without envy,
love without bile,
a life's work without guilt,
a poetry without attitudes.

The good days begin

The good days begin with light sun
bringing steel out of the frosty grass
and sweeps of parrots, bright as a fruit market,
are guessing that the air will not reach thirty
as they slow down, wheel, and count themselves.
Above them then, the cockatoos, even louder,
go compensating for their fate, their whiteness.
You can see how the noon will shape up, and the evening
begin, with its yellow styling and a sulphur edge on the
  dusk.

Smudged together, the new grass and the old
slept rough all night.
Now the cold picks them apart
like the strands of a rug
into cut, pale colours.
On the muddy bank above them
nettles grow, thick as strawberries.

Making Friends

There is the *festschrift*
to look forward to (if you're well enough),
and the quiet hours in the library
with the periodicals,
and the reconciling tots of whiskey,
and being driven to Cape Otway,
or Healesville or Cherokee
on a day's Outing.

You have grown into parenthesis.
You are no longer a patron.
You look brown, wired, abstract,
your jokes dawdle
and are easily capped.
Poetry, Vertu, Soul, are all
feats of the body: you know that now.
You make friends with the telephone.

Slender
as a splinter
the entry
to your cold flesh; with pincers
lift the flap of the breast
and reach in, and remove it
which, with all weaknesses,
divagations, abrupt slidings,
lived for me almost a whole life.
They take it out
as if it were a tumour.
They place it under the light.
It turns black, shrinking already.

Spring's Come

Spring's come, but not the cleanliness,
the wind brushes dirt in corners,
and the tiny black seed pods
seem covered with drapes of cobweb,
leaf-slivers, and dried matter,
the whole growing like a set of mobiles.
Time to enter, Botticelli-woman,
with the light on your shoulder
and the strong leg forward
protecting the sacred place.

Seasons

One page turns on to the next;
you hear them crick, burn,
their beautiful unfolded rhythms
curl down in caesuras

while out in the giant mist the traffic
burls like a toy, the fog settles down
head high like a weight of leaves
on midnight's streaks of colour

and you find, by the morning,
your clothes stick to you like clouds –
something no one planned, an autumn
too hot to burn leaves.

Summer has grown on to your skin,
summer grows from the moss like a jungle,
summer on the hook nets
the banana passionflower,

vine and tendrils one
thick freight of green
carried on windowpane and screens,
buffeting at the trellis

and on the poles a flask of wasps
hangs, starting to move downwards,
and the foreign breezes flick the garden
to a smell strong as vegemite,

strong and drying out. A dryness
of closures gone dark with the sun.

A Leaf from the Firestorm

City heat, that closed noise system
is clamped on you like canvas
while you stand after midnight
in your own garden, hosing
a leaf from the firestorm.

The water sparkling in the air
like bicycle spokes
makes a new thing out of it, smooth,
artefact, glossy as enamel.
It smiles on the grass. Behind you,
sizzling, new leaves from the firestorm.

Pound's Grave

The trumpet dwindled, and the bow wave
stopped at the battery of mooring-posts,
leaving us alone with death island
the graveside with its dwarf hyacinth
that rustles in near perpetual shade
beside the bay-laurel.
They are making up a ceremony.
In a hiss of speeches the sun begins setting;
the ambassadress leans her head
into her husband's shoulder. But Pound
has arranged quarters beyond ceremony
in a wilderness, from which the lagoon
twinkles with small furnaces, their roar
absorbed in the misty shrine of water.

They have spent your life in glass
framed by enamel, your eyes
hard as a camera; and if the mirror
shrinks in bitter ovals, thickens
or grows monstrous, its images
stay fixed and lunar
like a weight of fire.

Airletter to Craig Raine

Well, they are gone, and here must I remain,
this Elm Grove room my prison.

Room 101: the possums grate and groan
from the ash branches to the bricky roots
homing up to my ceiling.

The rats in tandem scratch the skirtingboard
neatly as if a watercourse
led them; they go by urine smell.

Twenty varieties of birds
snap the black seeds of the Queensland sapling;
autumn bushes bloom like hibiscus

and stretch out like flamingoes.
The grass grows its 5 o'clock shadow
under another tree,

and the heat tips more water
on black boles and dead leaves.

The rats in the wall are at it
so hard that, if they stopped, a third
eye would glow in the plaster –

Not even they want that,
for it might be the eye of a possum:
a demon, like them, given to trails

and territories. A quarter-mile away
a musk heavy as leafmould
washes the billabong

where tortoise and snake lay hidden
for months among comforting smells,
a sky full of craft materials.

They come at intervals

They come at intervals,
alone, walking the line,
or in twos, engineers, mapmakers, surveyors,
to plant their claws in the tiles,
to shake the house, rafter and doorframe.
As if sniffing food they poke at
small cracks, impermanencies in metal;
their medium is smell and weakness.

As they haul at the edges of roofs
they are dragging the tarpaulin
over my ears and my spirit
but I go on listening to them
in the bubbling of the gas-fire
surrounded by television mystery,
the Origin of Sounds.

Shine a torch upward, and
they will come down to the opening
and peer to it, looking into
the thin tray of cold light,

spin the ferrule on the coping
and they will shy like horses
as if a bugle had started them
rushing, and streaming like hair

towards some parade of the absurd
that will take all their claws and cunning

for nothing: for stopping and going
for being beaten off, and returning.

Moonlight Flit (of Possums)

Hear them at first light
like spirits leaving the house

they scrape and assail tiles
claws with the weight of shoulders
and mouths expostulating

like an escape of steam

SOFT WAR POEMS

1 *What do you want for this child*

What do you want for this child
(born stark as Jesus Christ, laid on new matting)?
If he's to be a poet, let him
not live in a place, or time, of war.
If she's to be a singer, let her
not be trained to sing war-songs.
The songs of armies drag on
scratchy as cicadas; the stories
are fit only for bad dreams;
the poems have been cut down
to a few mad, repeated lines.

2 *The War Season*

War times itself to the minute,
keeps high and low seasons,
is punctual as mealtime,
calling us all in
to take our places;

then, squeezing back into our breath
for a while yet, we see
that the young too have their moment
as the high-haunched mares their season,
a greed for war like love

makes the sun jerk in the sky,
the dead rise from the table,
and, suddenly, a lake white as frost
takes us. Voices are squeaking above us,
the crows fly into their season.

3 Naming of Peoples

In the superb reductions of print
it seems all right to call them
by names they never heard, or used:
The Halberd People, the Blue Spear People.
If peoples were still named after their weapons,
we would be called
the Projectile People, *or* Those Who Kill from Afar,
or Spitting Poison People, *or* Anthrax Minders.
On the great lowlands rugged with grass
we squat beside snout and muzzle,
we are growing moustaches
and learning laws of trajectory. Our films
are of painted, unrazed small towns.
On the jetfighter's broad jaw
we have painted: Homing Pigeon.

4 Synchrony

War has achieved its synchrony
as some late-working lovers
come, grunting, to their climax.
Enemies, regular as clockwork,
check watches, argue about time-scales.
Ripeness is all.

It is not only Reagan and some Russian
sitting, spruce or dour, near the red phones,
like someone expecting to hear 'Checkmate';
it's not only Beirut and the Israelis
challenging each other to the desert,
or Teheran and Baghdad burning in oil,
or Pol Pot and Hanoi, curved knives in the jungle:
we have always had these; and it's not only Castro
out on his own, always in great demand,
home barely one night in seven,
his study hung with skins from Africa:
we know leaders are performers.
No, it's the agreements they have typed and ready,
the machines they keep in leadfeatured rooms,
able to tell them all the world's times
like the consoles any amateur could play.

5 Glans Normalis

In the first dark of morning, when trees
skittered against the sky's wet weave,
its lights made a half-circle of distance,
each light hard as a stem; the garden green was raining.
Useless to plan defence while talking war;
for men of action, war's the tutorial.
The half-morning flicks on and off like midnight.
No good talking Defence while every News
keeps palping the gland of war: *Glans normalis*
swelling softly away there, in everyone's fancy,
and the warships nudge the swell of water
off Salvador, shaping up for Managua,
bumping like stock cars. 'Only manoeuvres',
just like kids mucking about. They steam and glide
in the glittery lead of the water,
Bay of Hope, or Spices, Resolution Bay,
all that: nosing blindly for their lost wars.

6 *The Arts of War*

To be taught the arts of war
you are taken into the gapped woods
and left there, alone. 'Stay three days.
After that, come out. Bring with you
anything you've killed.'

Easy. At dawn the crossing shadows
are thin as pencil lines. You move
as if you are living in a map,
carrying your thoughts into position,
making room for your body.

Until you are able to kill
every hour, if you want to.
Death has a cast of thousands,
each twig sound is a target. And you pack
life and future into three days.

7 Kildare

Winter wakes you in Kildare,
and all around the soft voices
have started gabbling: their subject
not crops, or horseflesh, but war.

What war can this be?
She's let her subjects die,
she's sent her warships sailing
down to the stark Antarctic

Where the planes like marlin glide
and men fall in their shadow
from the *Belgrano*'s side,
to the wave white as a floe.

But that's not what they mean.
Their voices snap, they quiver,
they are pointed like gundogs
at those massed deaths to come.

They see, light in the sky,
the feud of planets, hear
mountains wrenched from the sea,
they smell envy in grass.

Frighten me awake, good voices,
till I'm alive with fear.
Despairing men make bad prophets,
sleeping men poor soldiers.

8 Prime Minister

With the embassy raided,
the prisoners shot,
the TV cameras screwed shut,
then, in the HQ tent,
laughing and excited
as if at the Horse Show,
she could sit crosslegged on the grass
among her soldiers.

She is into machines.
Childlike as a patriarch,
she waves from the moving turret
after the guns have fired
their careful, neat trajectory:
Colonel Sidesaddle,
bringing back to her world
the rule of schoolboys.

9 *In the Pub*

Didja see how Mrs T. cut him
when he said that about the Falklands?
Not our business, said he.
Bloody cheek. But she was a match for him.
Always the lady. Sent him to Coventry
(as if there wasn't enough bloody Paddies there already).

10 *There are Always Some*

There are always some who run forward
and leap or fall on to the wire,
bugle or revolver in one hand,
the other fending off a sunburst,
and lie there, bloating the air,
soft as serge along the barbs:
and their comrades, later,
run forward, and crouch down, behind them,
taut dogs smelling at a covert.
These are the vanguard. They are
memorialised by a peculiar music.

11 *The machines all in line*

The machines all in line
the silos' rounded boles handsome
as plane-trees in the late light,
and the HQ's boundaries
going deeper into shadow.

       There's harmony,
also, in the great guns
canted on the hillside, where the copters
pirouette like schoolgirls: all caught
as in a picture-window
with the crowded modernist gaiety
of a toyshop, toy men
with clean metal eyelids,
shields taped to the chest
and shouldered batons, beyond whom the transports
rise and fall, stirring daylight
into a shir of dust.

       No god
could make it neater.
Only the protestors,
kicking weakly in the mid-distance,
assert indiscipline and smell. Primly
the guns gaze over their heads,
and set their sights on rubble.

12 *When It Comes*

When it comes,
squeezing our souls together in darkness,
you will not have chosen
morning or evening for it
and you will not be able to choose
whether to die indoors or out,
whether enfolding your children's bodies
or shredded, alone on black grass,
whether by sucking wind or fire,
by lightning bolt or crushed brainpan,
you will not even choose
whether to die as man or as woman.

Kerbside

The brick houses parked beyond the kerbside
are towed away into the fog
and the streets are left dark as burnt paddocks
through their new night. At the morning peak,
the cars pull into or out of driveways,
the leaves gather, the last
of the fog swims dry to the outskirts,
and the houses are seen neat as beds

in a hospital city. Like a poet
you've kept vigil with the thought of them,
fought off sleep and damp, feeling
a body weighed down
by cycles of medicines. A weeping hand,
an eye that draws deep lines
like furrows in the city skin:
the real nests in the surreal.

See how the road behaves. Each evening
the bitumen fumes up in mists, or kicks
like sparks off to the verges. Grows darker,
and the cars stopped at the lights
just off the freeway shudder, their motors
popping like grease. It has brought them
at devious speed down the same hill
to fight each other to the life,

thinking of engines that beget engines.
That's how I'd begin the poem:
Summer: sparkings of light everywhere;
now the noise I dread begins again.

Wittgenstein's Face

The skin texture, the bones
mimetic as music,
a strict system of plans
drawn for the spirit:
traced in, for example,
to Wittgenstein's grained face
that holds its aching profile
on the book's cover
till it seems, like Menuhin's,
a life's task: Is *it*
ugly or beautiful? A face
that would draw its questions down
the executioner's blade
looks out levelly, curt

with years of remissions,
and we see it as bone and flesh
at the moment of its invention,
not yet silenced; it looks out of itself
as if it presupposed hands
wrestling and talking
though wanting also to grope for
the rough edge of coat-sleeves.

The face is a closed kenning,
a riddle: *not death but dying
is an experience within life.*
Who has encoded this?

The Iceland Foxes

Boring as a cuckold
I find all the same that I need to
keep up with my night reading:
all the mind-triggers of our decade
from Historical Geography
to Dolphins, ESP, the Saints of Cornwall.
The first people to arrive in Iceland,
I read, found there only one mammal,
the fox. The Iceland Fox. Laying a musk,
giving birth, in the stench of volcanoes

while the impulsive, panicky invaders,
peering from ships bent like a riddle,
tried to see, to descry, wolf-stag,
lynx-bear, running jerkily on the sulphur slopes,
chased by half-men, screeching, with their knifestones
pelting the air. Eyes full of old habits.

Reading, imagining this, I say to myself:
Now, you've lasted through forty years
of universities, those correct pun-loving islands
with their soft grievances, their clubs, their baby-talk,
their low-rust landscape of the soul
where watchfulness is normal –
a gauntlet of islands – and you've come
into a new life, skilled in Agecraft,
free to think anything, tell any truth,
scotch any lie; and yet you sit there
doling your last years out to yourself
as if they were mogadon or heart-pills

while the organisation-persons hunt
confidently past libraries, carrying on
as if the jungles were not a form of culture
in which to invent new species,
not something learned and trained for,
but pristine things, native, imperative,
the most natural of enclosures.

Remember Mortality

Too much sweet talk. Remember Mortality,
that lovechild of the seminar?
Remember the years we spent
mulling over it (Mortality,
the great sub-text of poetry,
with all those classical subjunctives;
the big M; the complaint tradition,
the Praeparatio and Consolatio)
till it seemed to grow before us
with noble, sombre gradualism,
creased and leathery as Picasso,
but safe as a clutch of aunts and uncles.

It was all nonsense. Growing old
is done by quantum leaps,
collapses at the speed of light
leading to long declines,
showing like flushes
in your skin, under your nails,
planetary disputations.

Many a one has thought,
It is strange what is happening to me,
my life floating inside me
like a sprig, or a smell of islands,
my eyes fixed on a window
where the evening light is fixed forever,
the dream from which sleep comes.

So, what do you want me to write about?
The live past, the dead future?
Shopfront universities
the criminal zest of institutions
Satires of circumstance?
Friends bound in love by envy?
I will write of the future, which I know
with carnal clarity.

Suffolk, softly bristling with light
at every edge, a firm-tuned pipe,
almost undid me.
Good to be back in England,
I had written. And I stopped.
November hung on a few twigs
of shining berries. The wood,
fuzzy and unleaving, was *en brosse*,
soft, leafless, *en brosse*
Suffolk. And the angina squeezed
like someone strapping a case shut.

But winter's the test of things.
Dr Browne stood, considering
what I had asked him,
raw journeyings through midlands,
mountain switchbacks, flooded roads,
Wales, Wexford, Munster's coastline,
snow and sleety rain,
and said, Yes, you can manage that.
Now winter, travelling, overtakes us,
rides on the roof, stays alongside,
fills every crack with frost and mire.

And if you ask me,
Do you want, then, to be born again?
No, I was born once,
completely, in my mother's bed.
Who wants another's 'new life'?

Nothing Outside the Text

Quiet times.
The undergraduates gone.
Massa's at his conference,
four of you here alone.

Well, half-alone. The times
have made you diffident.
At the photocopier you ask
where Tom and Tina went.

And round the insecure corners
or from the roof you look
sharply at this unfruitful world
that can read you like a book.

'The camps'

'The camps', they would say, 'the camps',
'The way it was in the camps.'
If they had been in the permanent ice-cuts
of Siberia, any Siberia,
or worse, worst, the uncodable
smoke of Auschwitz,
even the later travel camps,
rest camps, transit camps,
camps for
resettlement, briefing, correction,
in the cold mud or summer dust,
it was always 'the camps'.
'We would not have put up with it
even in the camps'.
'In the camps
you wouldn't have known you were alive,
a man like you'.

That is what they taught him

That is what they taught him, so
that is what he wrote
to his wife after her miscarriage

'. . . the weather never lets up
and two of the ewes died yesterday in labour
I found them near frozen by the top hedge
I think about you and wish you were home
and I'm sorry I know it's a terrible disappointment
what did the doctor say about more children
did he say when you'd be coming home
I have to go and get them ready for milking
hoping this finds you well as it leaves me

                        Your affectionate husband
                        William McAuliffe

And she read it, as they had taught her,
and said to herself, O Will,
and the woman in the next bed asked
have you been hearing from your husband?
Yes, he says there are two ewes down.
Yes, it's bleak raw weather, we're better off here
in the warm, getting all the attention
not doing a hand's turn . . .

Your letters, written to praise and comfort,
have scared the wits out of me.
What God or hero could you have been addressing?
Who could be the subject of this nonsense?
And I clutch them in my pocket, as a clown,
under the high wire, grasps at his amulet.

The instructor of nightmares

The instructor of nightmares
smiled familiarly; gestured for silence:
'Now. The fourth lesson.
You are not the age you think.
You are older. Two years older.
You can follow the clues out
for yourself, if you can bring yourself.
Start here. She is not your mother,
you know, not really. Why does your father sob
each night in the dust of the spare room?
How do you think you came
to read so early? It is all clear,
unless you choose to be stupid. You are older, old,
you are not who you think. They are not
wives, but sisters. The animals of Eden
are still half-buried in the mould.'

How will civilisation last?

How will civilisation last?
Like mushrooms, sweated in season
out of the time itself: if not from strains
of civic virtue, maybe from the poems
that arrive, like letters, from refugees
over the frontiers or in the mountains,
from expatriates, in foreign cities,
the stateless and the expelled:
poems in the voices of soldiers,
old concubines and, well, poets.
Brief, but so homesick,
retching with longing
for the capital that denounced or expelled them,
its sheer style and its friendliness,
its birds and boulevards, that city

which hangs from their false memories
like brass lamps in the market.

My advice to the Dictator:
improve the mails. Start courier services.
Employ experts to sort the frayed letters
that will keep arriving, some addressed merely
Arcadia, or Home,
from the Siberias
of all countries.

Gulag I

To left and right, along the equator
the gulag spreads in the heat.
Long and broad that fungus
with its black pins heads, rafts of larvae
carrying their suck of spawn everywhere.

The gulag hooks in and commandeers
the shapes of mountains. It grows through dams.
Governors and slaves have fed into it
their most enduring treasure, their excreta.
Machines are strapped and bandaged to it.

The guards extend their guns on bare arms;
mosquitoes walk in their sweat.
The sun makes a bed for lice,
a dish for cockroaches,
skulls and ribs for the jungle.

These were men, these women,
whose flayed skin covered the sun.
Some died, rolled in their fever, some
escaped into the massacre,
some left scraps of poems in the midden
to send a few words
back to earth. Some choked on their prayers.

They stand beside us and point out
how it grows, spreads, north,
south, tundra, trades, chilled oceans,
a gulag for all climates,
even those that bind our continent
so hard, so anciently, so gently.

Public Poetry

O not 'public poetry', she said,
her cigarette making the quote marks,
let's drop these clichés. Women
have stopped thinking in those terms.

And she stared closely at me through the smoke

So that I had to say: But what's public?
What does public *mean*? Everybody
is tapping phones, government, media,
who whom. We have the score and report
on the Deadline Headline News every hour.
That one's the Leader, that's the horse.

Further,

Their Majesties and Royal Highnesses
are snipped from the weekend supplements
or stamped like recipes on biscuit tins;
that's public. All that was private

is gone into psychiatric wards, into eyes
dying in beds too big for them,
into bones flushed with radon,
or faded off like footsteps on gravel,
out of range of poetry.

Holiness of the Meat Trade

The health expert spoke on the wireless.
This is a small country.
It has eleven hundred slaughterhouses.
Perhaps a good many more.
Not all are supervised.
People have grown used to offal
in their streets, occasionally. They have learned
to step around it. Thank you.
That was Peadar Whatsit, the healthman.

Our butcher, the best in the whole district,
never closes on Good Friday. All that day
he's there, sawing and trimming
prime cuts for Easter. Faithful servant.
And the auctioneer yammers
over the cattlepens at Leinster Mart
on Holy Thursday. Is it all
some religious thing I'm not used to?

                But in the dark heat
                of the room at night, my heart jerking,
                I'm back in the saleyards, nine,
                ten years old, bringing
                our calves, my calves,
                my hand cupping their soft chins,
                my arm about their necks,
                glaring about me, tight with alarm
                as they're herded, mad with pride
                as the bidding moves up. Sad as Christ
                as I turn for home, with the few shillings
                and the empty halter. Economical.

Having revised our gods

Having revised our gods,
we are intently changing the animals:
re-originating species.
In cold practice rooms the shape-changers
graft fish on flesh, toad on mammal,
mating old enemies, for ever and ever.
We have proved there are no 'natures'. Now
to show there is no Nature. And
'the time is not far off when a human being
can decide not to be, biologically speaking, human.'
Didn't we manage that aeons ago?
And if nature, like god, is just a language,
there'll be lots, mainly the Past, to talk about,
but no names for the new animals.

Scientific Scanning

I can smell anxiety a mile away.
As soon as we got here I could see
this was an anxious town. Shop doors open,
some newly painted. Fanlights ajar.
I heard whistling from a roof. A girl said 'Morning!'
A man walked out of his house carrying bagpipes.
It added up to a high anxiety threshold,
as we put it. All of them
keeping to themselves. What we call recessive.
And the light walked straight through the main street
and wavered into a stand of trees.
I thought, don't tell me it's gone for good.

Letter Home

The barbarians occupy the Centre,
what they call The City,
Banks and Museums and the great churches,
they've brightened it all up,
painted the concrete platforms along the river,
filled it with windows that shine like mirrors,
burning-glass.

    You have to admire
their pride of race. They have no
identity problems. And they're born teachers.
They've ignored minor languages
and made everybody
learn Barbarian. So the place
is going ahead.

    I have been brought in
to learn to teach
Elementary Barbarian; it is a neat language,
a language of the future.
I have a small flat under the windows
with their one-way glass.

Portnoy's Revenge

I

Please address your answer to His Worship
said Leonard
Flanagan QC
who had noticed the beak was snoozing
*Your Worship I was just commenting
that some people might think the book,
while sprightly in some ways,
is boring as a whole . . . In fact, literary critics . . .*
I see, said His Worship. Yes, I see.
He had lost his pencil. He went back to dreaming
of the new friendly fundamentalism,
crowded churches, no reading, four tea-times a day.
I noticed that Flanagan QC
was humming to himself. What was he humming?
Dies Irae? 'In time of tea abundant'?

II

So you admit the book is disgusting,
Said Flanagan QC. It is your own word.
Disgusting as life is disgusting, said the Famous Witness,
and beautiful like life, full of despair and joy.
Would you call it filthy? Pornographic? Sexually arousing?
As Life is, said the Famous Witness. *Radically
filthy, pornographic, sexually ar . . .*
Aargh, said Flanagan QC, for God's sake.
The Famous Witness sat down beside me
and glanced at my averted eyes.
How did I go? he whispered.
I'll tell you later, I muttered, barely turning.
After a minute, he got up and left.
You should have finished the bloody book, I thought.

Said the Taxi-Driver

There's nothing like garlic and onions
they have no parasites
they are not molested by animals
if you rub them onto the right place, they heal.
I follow a diet that contains onions.

My old grandfather was a Billingsgate fishmonger
he taught me all these things.
Rub onion on the right spot,
he said, and you'll never have no trouble.

When I'm gardening
I always plant in the gaps.
With azaleas and some other trees
there are always gaps. Most people
won't plant in the gaps. I plant them all
with underground vegetables
onions and carrots, they have a flower,
but you don't eat that, so you don't mind
if the cat pisses on it. You just throw it away
and you know the underground fruit
will do you good.

The tree I'm most careful with
is the magnolia, I've got three of them.
They're a lovely tree, the magnolia,
they flower in winter and drop all their leaves at once.
You know what I like about magnolias?
All those leaves fallen together
they make great mulch.

Hear how the Irish speak pentameters

Hear how the Irish speak pentameters
(I do, myself, sometimes), catch up the pulse
That's arguably the true gait of the breath.
Today I heard the RTE presenter
Say this, while introducing Fluters Five,
'They learned their trade in front of marching banners,'
Then, of the man who partnered them on *bódhrán*,
'He learned his music in a different field';
And no word of religion at all:
Just as it should be in the world of song.

Now that I'm speaking of this regal mode,
If mode it is, this opened pulse of joy,
Let me tell how it thrives on opposites,
Left, right; soft, hard; quick, long; the speech of drums
That echo but don't rhyme, are one prolonged
Echo or train of echoes down the line:
'The man who heard it coming round the bend
Has heard it also buried in the mist,
Clacking in leaves, or muffled in stone walls.'
They're like a family, no two the same.
The tricks of sound they play are all betimes.
We know the iamb; what's the iambic line?

Gulag II

They write out scraps of poems
on old wrapping paper
and plant them in the earth
close as possible to the wire.

They hear the Amis are coming,
the liberators,
but for their mind the poems
will have taken glossy wings
and flown to the west before them.

Even skimming the lowest wire
untrained poem, go
with a full throat.

No. They know the poems are buried
without wings or breath.
Even if their own starved bones
are led out through the gate
the poems will never move.

'They are buried, Vasil,'
in the black Hour of the night,
'buried like memory.'
'Yes, but so close to the wire
they might jump with our mind
skimming the lowest strand.'

Perfect Pitch

Could perfect pitch have saved us,
or learning the art of closure,
or cadence, or deep tuning,
or the Theory of intervals?
The older I get, the more
I think: In the next life
I will be a maker of music,
not bothering with words.

Except that they cause each other,
and cornet and flute in the smoked air
will leave the dragonish curvings of a tune
that some will sing along with, some
nod at, listening, with closed laughter,
thinking What is this language? What is its grammar?
It might happen like strutting a funeral,
Didn't he ramble. O didn't he ramble.
or *Fa'en like flooers o' the forest,*
and horn and oboe is mimicking a voice
just when I have fallen into silence.
The shapely silver cry
that stops the mind. *A' wede awa'.*

Still when I look at the usual
order of things, Venus downwind
from the rising moon, with a clear line
between them, down which you could roll a ball,
the pinetrees set up as masks before them,
and, under them, everything that burns with life
running and dying: the bodies scrawled in Athens,
tanker on tanker on fire in the gulf,
property still theft, all the earth's chemicals
crawling with death like woodlice, I would not want
to say anything, for fear of saying too much.
But noticing how the melody drifts through
like a private joke,
I would want at most to station the oboe,
the clarinet, or the pipe's chanter
in some clear spot
to curve the rise of the cadence towards Venus
but happy to touch the moon.

UNTITLED SERIES

I

Now the summer winds do blow
I drink, and sicken for the snow

The days grow longer till they snap
And Aunty groans from nap to nap

Blowfly's boom, cicada's grate,
Remind me of the truth I hate,

The truth some hide, and some deny,
And some, so vain, hate more than I:

Golden girls and prefects must,
Like old nerve-cases, come to dust.

II

The arse licker
averts his eyes

The champion of New Theory
looks over his shoulder

The jolliest leader
has books on weathercocks

And Bilke is a self-confessed
aristocrat.

III

The mass-rapist and murderer was convicted on Tuesday.
'He was always good to me,' says his wife.
'He is a shy man, basically insecure,'
Said a friend who is minding his two retrievers.

A Professor's role is Academic leadership.
Professor Hipp led from the front, running
through the minds of his juniors like a brainstorm.
'He always treated me fairly,' said Tom Bilke,
who is still chuffed from his promotion;
'I can understand how some people found him abrasive.'

There are people who say that to all the victims;
Satires of Circumstance ferment in the soul.
Even the most talented of you must have known
that choking cut across the windpipe when you think,
Will I speak out? And of course it's too late.

IV

The mountains walked back in clear,
and the snowflakes that avoided your warm body
dived at the ground. You brought out
strong eddies around each other.
The street-lights gently swelled
and dripped like sponges.

In the windings of my bed
nothing of this scene is shed.

As the sun comes into focus
we get the midday sound,
birds winding themselves up
on the iron fastening of a gable
to close their mouths against winter.
If this planet has a music,
the air is moved into the key of pearl.

In the fortunes of my bed
I remember all that's said

before these winter lives,
these songs no bird believes.

V

In switches of cold the winter goes
putting a layer of new sensations
over its memory of mildness;
birds and stray dogs,
anything that uses waste places,
pick over its livelihood.

What keeps me inside
is the pain buckled like a belt
that can't be broken,
that bends me over
like a waxworks figure,
Beckon, sir, I pray you,
Nay, Dickon, let me there gainsay you.
Stiff as the robin standing, glooming.

The cold is still cracking like branches.
The sound *preeewhitt* up the chimney
(Small bird or sudden fire?)
the stoat bounding on the snow ridge
is neat as Alan Ladd running,
his head like a longjumper's
erect for landing, for the big one.
Nothing is *faux naif* here.

That odd ticking in my heart
comes out in bruises
linked near my breastbone,
I stopped to touch them by the wall,
and I couldn't even tell the doctor
what was bothering me,
I was so bloody tired of it all.

VI

Nightmare of a Chair Search Committee

How nice to get Dr Forter.
How nice indeed, my dear;
He writes for the Saturday papers,
He's a Grade A mountaineer;
besides, as a sort of bonus,
he'd be away two-thirds of the year.

What about this Ms Avaporto?
Is anyone pushing for her?
Avaporto, is that Italian?
O I don't think there's much to fear.
She comes with a reference from Billitt.
Let's wait and play it by ear.

Ralph had a letter from Harold.
He's on leave, I think, in Trier;
there's no one in Europe. Of course not,
but Oxford is far too dear,
though that young woman at Merton
may bring out her book this year.

Do you think we could get an American?
Someone not too queer?
No, no I didn't mean that. But someone
trained as a Conferenceer,
Someone from Princeton or Harvard
(Yale's on the way out, I hear).

And so on, and so on, and so on,
for more than nine-tenths of the year.

Tips for Performers

Learn to speak of yourself
in the third person.
'That's what Sumner Brones is all about.'
'What next for Brones Sumner?'
You sound like a parcel
for special delivery.

Don't entirely abandon
the royal plural.
'We look forward to further challenges.'
'That has never really concerned us.'
You sound like an answering service
on a half-pissed telephone.

Give in. Follow the fashion.
Use the nobs' pronoun.
'I wanted it for she and I.'
'That was the trouble with he and they.'
You'll sound like someone reading
Debrett with his false teeth out.

Teaching German Literature

I teach German literature, and this is how it goes:
Schiller, Boll and Holderlin, and everybody knows
that Bertolt turned on Thomas Mann and punched him on
  the nose,
and Goethe married Clara Kronk and Clara married
  Wagner.

Hardy is a Proximist, and Philip Larkin hates
walking past the neighbours' children hanging on the
  gates.
Keats was orphaned, Donne was bent, and Shelley went
  out drowning,
and Wordsworth married Sara Dronk and Sara married
  Browning.

T. S. Eliot, marvellous boy, grew up with a mitre;
even in dark Russell Square you wouldn't find much
  brighter,
Furster Rilke knew a duchess, Trudi von Bachbeiter,
and Mara married Pablo Yeats and Pablo never married.

The greats of German literature are in the dressing room,
Lotte Lenya, Suky Tawdry, fending off life's gloom,
Hans Otto Eller Manzenberger smiling at his poem,
and Clara married Leslie Liszt and Leslie married Magna.

And Goethe married Clara Kronk and Clara married
  Wagner.

Piccolo Spoleto

In foreign places. Fitzroy, Northcote. The street party
for Act One, barbecue and dancing,
the judging of the balloon sculptures.
Second act: the Carpathian State Circus
in St Paul's Cathedral, Jasper Monologuist,
from Boston New Jersey, at the Marmalade Factory.
Fitzroy? He said. Is that an Indigenous . . . ?
No, Jasper. What about Northcote?
No, that's foreign too. They're both foreign.
We are learning to govern ourselves
but it's not been easy. The indigenous accents
are very like Cockney. Hoopla Stall,
that's Hungarian. Not to go on about it,
but we are a mixing bowl
of four hundred nationalities and six temperaments.
As our founder said, scratching his wallet,
this is the place for a salad. Enjoy. Enjoy.
Even that's not been easy.

My Mother's Anzacs

Take your pick: the roan in the moody paddock
year after bloody year, and the dawdling cows,
or the grand tour, the Pyramids, the Last Post,
the smack and harness sounds of rifles,

mates running and kneeling up in the sand
where their turds were buried,
stumbling up over their own handholds,
joking about it, getting close enough

to hear the bristle of the Turkish oaths
when they reared, close enough to link blades
or to see one another grinning
at this Other. That'll stretch their cods.

Back home they were raging against my father.
A male bonding, mate? A coming of age?
Your menstruation? No, it was my mother's
myth-time, the openeyed failure of her girlhood.

There was the sea. And footholds
stepped into the land, the dung-coloured
long bathing place, its beach, slopes,
gullies and escarpments, all the way
up the plateau, everywhere
was our army, lying, shooting, shovelling,
a land-covering, black as treacle.

A few yards from the front of it
the Turks, laid out in their army
with their weapons, breathing, eyes scared like us,
lying in fissures, on the slopes,
a sand and rock covering
stretched black as treacle, all the way
to the bathing place, the footholds. There was the sea.

And their hessianed dead,
thrown in front of them, falling apart
inside their tunics, the swaggerers in puttees
neatly darkened in the shitty sand.

Just when these others have stopped singing
and doused their cigarettes, and inched forward
to be thrown up the slope as up a wall
to die humped like vines on terraces.

Her slow eyes will guard them coming back
into her album, shapes caught in a brownout,
implausibly high-shouldered, hair combed sideways,
bringing a paleness back to everything.

We are seeing the death of photographs;
slouched heads curdled on the paper, light
pushing in at the corner of the eyes;

We are hearing the death of songs
which die being sung by the wrong people
in prim accents that slide off 'shit', or 'gravel';

We are laughing at the death of death-jokes,
jokes about impotence or bowels,
and the home-front, and the warp of their own faces.

And then, dead, they taught you what life is,
in the risquéd jokes and boyvoiced kitchen singing
in your fist pressed to your midriff, and your legs
   bleeding,
and how to forget what you can't photograph:

almost everything: your staring eyes,
the half-scared pleased attacking voices,
or the comic slouch of their shoulders on parade,
or the years going brown as they do,
that drive a pinpoint deep into their eyes
resisting the camera till the last minute;

And the young women left, chalked with sunlight,
prudish, laughing, tightening their hair,
who, married elsewhere, found year after year
their songs bewildered by a photograph.

Taught: the sun that fadeth everything
browns on the wrists and foreheads of the dead
that lie here, twisted, softening and spent,
that went to war for songs
having stepped into and out of photographs.

And fade our voices, scattered, distant, potent,
furred from the creek's light,
but full of noise as animals
not needed till tomorrow,
free to imagine memories of their own.

HUNGER-STRIKE

> **Warrior:** 1. One whose occupation is warfare; a fighting man; in eulogistic sense, a valiant or an experienced man of war. Now chiefly *poet.* and *rhet.*, exc. as applied to the fighting men and heroes of past ages and of uncivilized peoples.
>
> *Shorter* O.E.D.

To Redefine 'Warrior'

    Through this season
of hot clouds, you have needed
to redefine 'Warrior': One
who makes war, with no weapons
but the sticks of his forearms,
the electric pain of his body
in his cell, away from the air
his family breathes, drenched with sweat
of armed men, with machines,
robots, automatics, clockbombs,
hijacked milk-lorries,
sprayguns and knapsacks of gas,
plastic bullets, shields, visors:
For the armed man is known by his tools,
but a warrior by the death of his terrors

and of their monstrous dream prototypes:
tortured heads, with holes large as faces
opened in them; a corpse hung at the ford;
a serf enduring the thousand lashes;
statues fighting; a masked man
beckoning between the armies;
a comrade lasting into his sixtieth day;
a lark, as he said to himself, at the window
but caught, crying, by the foot, in black wire.

Bobby Sands: One

>   Now he is laid on the sheepskin rug
>   so that his bones will not burn him,
>   pads are put on his heels
>   against the bedsores. He is blind
>   and deaf. The pain they told him of
>   jolts its thin current
>   into every movement. His teeth
>   protrude like the bones of a dead man.
>   He is dying for his word. *Geronimo*.
>
>   They would not let him alone.
>   Day and night they came and went
>   stirring his pallid shadow,
>   interpreters of his dying.
>   Day and night he hung on the wire,
>   his curled body outlasting them
>   till they fell silent; 'he was the piper
>   walking in the front of battle'.
>
>   Then, he died in a clean place,
>   crooked, on the waterbed, the Pope's
>   crucifix proudly beside him, his mind
>   open as a galaxy.
>   *Le dur desir de durer*
>   saw him buried as Geronimo.

Sands: Two

>   But, before that, he was lowered
>   into the deep trough
>   of others' wills, his wire thin bones
>   buzzing with speeches, lights
>   thick on his shrinking face,
>   died badgered with help,
>   not hearing
>   the faraway words his mother
>   spoke to the microphone.

For her the hard thing
must have been keeping her eyes down,
her lips steady, while blurting out
what they had said to each other: 'We talked
about old times . . . when he was at school
. . . and in the youth club . . .'

This was the time when
everyone came to talk at him
and to come out and tell the world
what he wanted, and why
he should/should not want it
          [But he wanted not to give up,
          and not to die either. Geronimo.]

The sky was full of mouths: except the father,
who said nothing, the brother,
who was an arm to lean on
for the sister, who could not hide her eyes,
and the mother, all large
unweeping features, and going in,
and coming out, and going
only to come back next day
to the reporters husking like bees:
'How is he today?' 'He's dyun.'

Francis Hughes

Colonel, press your cap down hard
or keep your fingers in your belt,
searchlights and men in every yard,
the tree beside you red with haws,
Saracens in the windgreen lanes,
the day they bury Francis Hughes.

Is this the corpse you hate so much,
that awesome boy, going to Mass
on a weekday morning in Bellaghy,
loitering so the late dews pass
along his footstep to the door,
thinking the land's his own, perhaps?

Go to your tea, sergeant, trooper,
his shadow follows you with scorn
now that you've lowered his starved face
deep in the ground where he was born:
the long-eyed kinsman drumming on it
tunes you will never learn or bear.

Raymond McCreesh

    Weeks later, it was his face
    that loomed on the hourly news,
    tilted back, fragile, laughing.
    To whom someone said, on the 58th day,
    do you want a drink of milk?
    He was blind now. He said, I don't know.
    Batlike his brain in and out
    of his body-shape, the mind's landscape
    entering and leaving sun and shade.
    For days, on the wire services,
    in press statements, they took his name:
    Do you want a drink of milk? I don't know.

And they talked of his family
as if he were straining
to leave some mad priesthood, or to break
some taboo of the townland,
and the people he loved would not let him.
                Eloquent assassins,
                Oxbridge men, Sandhurst men,
                I am almost too ashamed
                to mention your shame.

Interlude for Exploration

>Standing at the microphone,
>he shot his cuffs and said, earnestly,
>'Good God, we're not barbarians,'
>while the other railed against all violence
>booming, 'kill the killers.'
>None of them is a barbarian
>they are all against violence
>which (let us be quite clear)
>they totally and unequivocally reject.
>What they *do* support
>is the police and the army
>and Saladins in the closed streets
>and plastic bullets at walking schoolgirls
>and blackened faces waiting in the darkness
>after the local dance; and the spacemen
>on each corner, with their guns cradled,
>and the knowledge that the Opposition is with
>   them
>
>and that the Bishops, who hate violence,
>will ask no hard questions, and the columnists
>will be as full of similes as the poets,
>lightheaded (this way, that way)
>and Oxford will debate measure and process,
>and the *Tablet* moral or some other theology
>(all against, utterly against violence)
>and the sun will rise in the West
>if we want it, for we are dying
>as much, but not as fast, as
>their unarmed prisoners.

Interlude for Execution

>On the waste ground where they shot him
>two or three birds fly up
>flapping, as if the air's too heavy.
>The ground is drifting with lead.
>Nothing grows. Vanished even

the permanent knuckles of the plane-trees,
and the people who heard him screaming
can grow nothing inside,
and can say or think nothing
while they wait for the suicide hour
flashing with law and order.

Patsy O'Hara

Fourth, Patsy O'Hara. We had seen his sister
moving from door to door,
from taoiseach to taoiseach*,
with her unanswered face,
while all the time he sat, with hunched beard,
in his bugged, photographed cell,
waiting till they would make him
carry his body down the Creggan
moving in procession
slow and quiet as a milkman
while the young boys in their staring thousands
drummed their heels on Derry's walls.

Joe McDonnell

who said, and became famous for it,
'I've got too much to live for,'
and said later (or it may have been Kiernan
    Doherty),
'I don't want to die over a food parcel,'
died on my birthday. It was almost exact mid-
    summer.
The black flags at Walkinstown roundabout
were held up for hours by the waiting faces
and the midges at Phoenix Park
stung even the feckless Spanish students
in hot moist green that seemed to grow warmer
in the encroaching shadows

And Martin Hurson on Grania's birthday.
And Kevin Lynch and Kiernan Doherty
died shortly after the Commission
had failed to solve the English.
    (That question of the ages:
    How do you solve the English?)

And Thomas McElwee, the shy-looking cousin
countryman, a proper devil for cars;
whose eight sisters carried his coffin
into the silent crowded roadway,
then on, with other bearers, into
the roaring graveyard, where
the whole countryside swayed in late summer.

And another long-eyed northerner
enrolled in their love compact.

---

*Taoiseach is the Irish for the head of government.

DIGGING IN

I

People are terrified of their souls.
The lowslung pub at the crossroads
goes at night into small huddles
at the bar, on the torn vinyl,
with sparse lights nodding in the bottles.
The brief pagan gulf of time is nearing.
The six hours of full daylight
are hoarded like candles,
shining dull as candle light.
You light a fire. It leans against the winter
with the primitive gesture
of a woman squatting,
grinding earth. The hot ash
at the door cheeps like a fledgling.

II

Tractors catch by day, your heart
rouses and strains all night
as the wind's after-torrents
pour into and out through
those tubes of landscape.
And suddenly midnight
is howling from the north,
dealing the slates off
like hands of cards.

III

Your dream was a rats' tunnel,
you were inside it.
For days you drank in wind, inhaled wind,
and the mares made unsettling runs
at their invisible barrier,
streaming out, the scared coven,
on to a land skin torn like netting.

The children had stopped already
hungering for the snowdrifts. They hung about
weightless as the weights of a clock,
snow filled the rooms with darkness.

IV

You were there while the house swerved
into its quarrelling nights,
filled with lintlike curtains and coarse
eyelashes of smoke, an engine
manoeuvring its nightlights
into the white flux. Caught bags of turf,
heaved churns of water
through the stable doorway,
the kitchen fire straining
to rescue more than it could see,
the stove cracking silently apart,
the panes worked free from their lead strips,
the tall front rooms
arrived finally at the colour
they were to keep all winter
as the wind sliced them, a razor
cross-cutting down a turned face.

V

Like walking in a salthouse,
sniffing and coughing up whole mornings,
trying to re-order last night
by the weird line of fire on Brewel Hill,
whose trees heated like iron bars,
so crimson you could smell the resin,
yet windless, utterly silent.

VI

Dogs cleft their tongues.
The ground, where it showed through,
was seal colour,
everything except snow was sinking.
Stars clashed on a stiff axis.
A step would break invisible spokes.

NOTES FROM BLACKHALL

I

Promiscuous starlight, touch nothing
you can't hold. The object
bends into shadowy scooped fissures
where damplines intersect.
The stone spreads like granules of water,
the water leaves glue of lime.

As I walk home, up between the trees,
the lee-black herds
huddled in engine mists,
I see him, and I turn startled,
why does the cock pheasant
nest on the ground, in the ivy?
Why does he scare so late?

II

All day the fires were stark
on the ridge of the ploughed land.
Next day the saw comes
stirring and sapping, a taut side
lopping every tree. Then
more fires, nearer the house.
A bit here, a bit there,
the world disappears.

And you are into the cold thrill
of uncovery, land cleared of its humus,
multi-coloured, cropped, paled,
waiting the harrow of evening.
By the end of the week they'll find
the white kitten's head.

III

Hermes

Tomorrow they'll light fires in the stubble
to run forward a bit, double back, sparking
and tittering. You'll think they must have lighted upwind,
it burns so small. With no flame. And next morning
the paddocks are ploughland, crudded brown, until,
by the straw light of evening
it is longstretched, wavering, beige as with heat,
full of jays, combed but unbroken;

the whole sign-system changed;
and more leaves have slid down by the ivy
on the wet ground. In a few more days
the owl will start being seen in the upland,
floating his own dark patch of air behind him,
and the god of boundaries
begins to walk the mearing of the ditch
between clodland and pelting grass.

IV

The Sun and the Owl

The sun, dead centre on the roadway,
tapped, huge as a harvest moon,
deliberating, loosing slivers
and stream-showers of light, to blind
everything that moves
straight towards it. Turn left, into lanes,
wheels dripping phosphorous,
to hear the thin tenor owl preparing,
ahead, its night of hooked noise,
starting . . . sole . . . sole . . .
passageways it will never finish
behind the tower's stone windows.
It's just on Hallowe'en. The windows
are pinched in like mouths
that have eaten, mumbling their names.

V

Sunday Shooting

It's Sunday shooting here,
low hedges, bracing air;
a brace of gunmen wade
along each fractious road,
bird-crazed, to the damp
preserves of bog and swamp.
This is The South; up there
in a headier hemisphere
where church and state are one,
it's black suits in the sun.
Here, in Flood's long paddock,
that has no gate or lock,
the brooding thoroughbreds
won't even raise their heads
and hen or cockbird sways
home by the reddest ways
a few yards from my stick,
Sabbatical, prim, eccentric.

VI

Hunter

We are neighboured by all sorts.
She rides her hunter down the avenue,
the shaven stallion cropped and dressed,
his hocks awash with light.
His hooves strike gravel as if
testing a cauldron, he spreads,
his shit droppings thick as chestnuts.
Monday they'll draw near Ballitore,
over Pike Bridge, where the United Men
in '98 scattered the troopers. Pony,
thoroughbred, half-draught, blood on blood,
safety in numbers.

VII

Great Sport Sunday

On the fast stretch from Naas
the Kildare foxhounds go past, lolling
from their ventilated truck;
their tongues are out and running
Yub Yub Yub Yub
they're off to Narraghmore

where the village, half-watching, turns
quietly, and talks of itself:
'Ye'd great sport Sunday' 'That we had.'
Coursing the live hare
in McCall's field. (Close by
the undiagnosed cattle
wheezed under their illnesses.)
The days warmed; the mink
squeezed their way up river
to the lamb's throat and hot intestines.

VIII

Settled In

His VW, haybales strapped on
to its waddling back,
goes low as a badger
back into the evening. The horses
turn to their night of female straw.
The fox draws Byrne's hill,
coming slowly down
to the oldwoman smell and the bantams
and the heelheaded dog
by the forge snapping at Mars or Saturn:
the edges of their world
folded in, immobile
as the crick of flesh or linen,
and the centre humming with
loneliness, their sole articulated purpose.

IX

Nurture

The trunk stripped of its bark
in one long shuddering blast
stands; a blurred white;
but the ivy already fastens
on a single small black knot
of wood, tight as a nipple.
The strands creak softly. The air,
cool eddying, hairfine,
stays upright.

X

With your standard heart-murmur
and corrugated eyelids
and your walking stick
to slash at the undergrowth
and prod the slimed pebbles,
you are the melancholic
with his arts of memory:
you see the earth passive
as if it had felt nothing
for aeons, not even the worm-crazed birds
last week, in the broken cold,
going up and down on it.

Natura Naturans

Rilke said of her,
with the usual grand regretfulness,
'Nature knows nothing of us.'
But this pregnant mare with her low head
and propped legs, mooning by the electric pole,
tricked by her hormones,
knows me; and the gamebird knows me enough
to walk the few steps before me.
It is Rilke they know nothing of,
and nothing of Proust, either, or Sartre.
They hear the engines in the next paddock
run, shudder, crackle,
like a tree falling. They know
it is not a tree.

These new scarlet blotches
on the backs of my hands,
are they Nature? or some new
vellum-art of the skin?

The Coven

I

Give them their due, the coven,
mares who come closer in to form
irregular small circles, and inquisit
the most myopic objects.
Their heads like swollen flowers
nip at the air, from neck
hooked carefully over neck.

The brooders stand, spare as herons,
under the trees. They are tree colour.
When the grass leads them forward,
they become hay colour.
Everywhere, networks of camouflage
that use up mane, tail,
and lowering eyes.

The winds all winter held their closed faces
that could be seen waiting, as locusts do,
to break open at midnight, to be born
in the raw stable air
so the children of their bellies
might go back with them, glass-eyed,
trotting feebly, to stamp with the coven
and run downwind like hares.

Making strange, they will run
at the fall of a leaf, the trivial crash of a motor,
a marsh-bird ripping,
or at nothing.
The strings of the wind let them touch
each other, lightly as grassblades do.

II

Mrs B. gripped in her cardigan,
watched them. Anne P. stood her stallion
up to the fence, beside his lead-pony,
while seven of the twelve snuffed towards him.
'I thought some of the dry ones might give a show,
But it's only the biddies in foal
that have come over.' Well,
what's a man to say? Fiona,
jacket collar up to her chin,
walked quickly, swishing the halter.
She'd have the dragging-out
of each one, rolling till the straw steamed,
and each, it seemed, would peak close to midnight.

Louisa Stewart is Foaling

Winter has coloured the straw dark as sweat.
Louisa Stewart is foaling. Nothing keeps clean;
but the stable rats, if they're watching, do it quietly
at the sight of the mare named for the gentry foaling.

Lord Waterford is dead, so the rebels sang
in '98, and most of the Beresfords
have gone, to hell or London. But they've come back
as magistrates, bosses, titular studmasters.

The corners of our house look cold as iron;
the cobbles of the yard shine hard as an axle
between the midwinter stars. She is grunting. Strange
vanity, to name your racemares after yourselves.

And the devil makes his bed, the song went on.
Sweat-oiled, named for the grandee's family,
Louisa Stewart, stifflegged on her side,
lies foaling; her head wags; the great damp arse

heaves up and down on straw. Noise grinds the yard
where the blind mare, who's not in foal this year,
stretches her neck, twists out her head like rope
for what is listening with her. A thread of wireless

harpmusic out the window, warm as twined fingers.
In the one acre we have the bard's triad,
music, fertility, blindness,
the whole of life: and Louisa voiding her colt

with the ropes tied to his forelegs, and three of us
haul on the rope, heavy as bellringing,
our legs braced, clutching each other's waists,
to force out blazed forehead and marble eyeball.

O she did it well without fuss. Cool as the gentry.
I think if I go out into the forest I'll hear
in the long paddock the whole coven running,
mares and foals together, in startled bursts

set off by her unheard breathing in the darkness;
and now they are streaming down over the ditch
in a delighted joke of unity. Louisa Stewart,
who did her job in style, will need clean straw.

The Curragh in Cold Autumn

The punters in the stand spoke like spitting.
'Fockin',' they said, and 'fockin', eh, fockin','
through the fagends hoarse as eucalyptus.
In the Members this speech was more drawn,
less committed, as the fieldglasses hung
below the halves of whiskey. High Style,
by Interest out of Nonchalance.
You'd almost think they'd won without betting.
All the same. The wintry wind, the air
unravelled like a rope, belted so hard
it sliced clods from the ground. And the three-year-olds,
slicing too, came awkwardly, their silks
rain-coloured, no-coloured, in the blast,
their shoulders struggling, down the interminable straight,
their hooves dripping, as if running at us
from the black caves of County Meath.

Sheela-na-Gig

The wintry keen goes. He has cut a
scythe line through the dry berries
and scraped stone-dust from the *cunnus*.
Now two men, squatting in the rain,
are measuring her
with red rubber, saucy as latex
as though for a young bride's coffin.

The Lake

A lake thin with reeds, an aluminium
light coming and going on its margins,
a road that needs to be explained.
'The books say she had it built in the famine
to provide work for the people.
The people say she built it
so she could bypass the village.'
Then, as if reaching the core,
'One thing you could say of the Irish people,
they were never loyal to their masters.'
No. And they lasted like the reeds,
the small rushing river, the dead verges,
the evening that holds up the black air.

Many here, you can see that,
would have bad dreams. As soon as the scalp
and bone lift off in sleep, the sheep's-
foot will tap on the drumlin,
and the ghosts of stillborn
animals and fallen men come out
and stare, circling among us,
as long as the moonlight lasts
in the dead centre
of the tilting field.

But, for once, that time, the evening
was a black frame; and where
the green rushes glimmered
by the lakeside, the sunset struck
openly, as if the Electricity
flashed all at once, for the first time,
in every green rise, each cottage,
pond, and thick monkish marsh.

Thus like a scalp
the drumlin lifted; all swam
in the teemed water, all
with electric weight struck
the rising air with foreheads of beasts.

Triads

3 Things not to be expected

> Patience from a drunk woman
> Humour from a drunk man
> Understanding from armies

3 Things to be forgotten

> A stillborn sister
> A grandmother's long hair
> A nubile mother

3 Impossible things

> To shape the air
> To civilise money
> To comfort a paranoiac

3 Fragile things

> The cool of sunrise
> Peace in the fowlyard
> The throat of a statesman

3 Unacceptable things

> A dirty dentist
> A timid bookie
> A prayerless priest

3 Lost things

> Poems by heart
> Water without acid
> Sleep without fear.

BIRTHDAY SUITE FOR SEAMUS HEANEY

I

You were brought up to bear gifts.
It is something we learn in the womb,
as I, too, learned a little
from my straight-haired mother;
it has to do with courtesy
and the keeping of birthdays.

So, gift-balancing, you walk forward
with that look of the boy
(intent, impersonal, round-shouldered)
at the Offertory of the Mass,
handling the elements,
wine, water, linen, cruets, for
a time-crazed traveller.

Northern glints of the mezzogiorno.
Orphic runes. We learned it
once and for all going
round and round in the inimitable
untorn perimeter of waters,
being pushed against by music.

II

So many ways of making music. One
sits, with knees pursed,
neat as a Protestant, and gets on with it,
playing to some invisible fixed point;
one puts his cheek against the fiddlehead
with eyes closed, like a Catholic,
and lets it come in through his bones,
a sound like simple warmth.
In love impersonal as a birthday.

III

The Mohock mountain, with its pine forest
as background, the air lead-blue
for dozens of gulls to dip bright as wire
in the thermals of sunset, three geese
assembled their triangle
carefully, above Rathfarnham, pulled west
away from the front porches, the cement dust,
the Owendoher crippled on its damp bed,
the schoolgirls pouting and crossing
in the cul-de-sac, the boys
tossing and turning on their bicycles,
with the special dull
clumsiness of daring children.
The blue light squeezed them all flat,
and over all the raindrops,
unfallen, gleamed black as an alloy.

In late April, snow blinded the gardens
between the currant and the cherry blossom.
None of them had died yet,
the men on their pallets
pulling their strength into a smaller circle.
And if children died under armoured wheels
or father and son in a shower of milk bottle glass,
or a mother with her clipboard on a stranger's doorstep,
it was all, hot, in the future's
hot unsorted entrails,
filling the mid months of the year
while the geese barracked from the west.

For now, I'd merely scrawl in the notebook
3 geese. Triangle. Striding west. Leaving.

IV

Poets, with their room-bound acts,
their room-soft fingers,
are aimless movers. But the piper,
thin as a coat-hanger,
when he squares himself onto the chair,
with cuddled pipes, is bound by nothing.

He is hearing touch. Eyes drawn right back
into the syndicate of our memories,
he sets the body lurching with music,
giving those small irregular
heavings, inch by inch forward,
as the whorls of his fingers
press in the whorls of the tune.

So little self: like a foetus
surrounded by a heartbeat, tumbling
towards a birthday. I always thought my father's,
three days after yours,
a blundering day, a middle of dark autumn
aberration, hard to feel proud of.

It was the anniversary of Culloden
where thirteen Scanlons died
a drab long way from Shanagolden,
paying some outdated blood-dues,
dug into grass for Bonny Scotland,
the northern springtime of the year.

V

    The daisies are tough in the greensward
    nothing cuts them down
    their pale red lids stay turned outward
    to the pits of the town

    where the city air, moist, swollen
    under the flap of weather,
    draws out the sting of death.
    In Long Kesh it's colder
    and the gaol's edge is clear.

    The bodies lie in a hard chapel,
    the rot on hands and face
    grows brown. The blood turns liquid
    towards the camera. Look.
    Here. The death of place.

Unbending daisy. Its god, averting
death, primes it again,
the brute small flower full of instinct
lasting without strain;

But look up, and the Summer's
gone, that had no ending,
our throat and our soul gone, our purpose
gone, that grew no language,
that heard no subtle drum,
no grace, and no friendship.

VI

What is my country? It is threaded
through you like a coat, the million
kindred answering *Who is my neighbour?*
It is nursling, and close to hand.
See, at the door to the kitchen,
this small girl, on planted feet,
lowering with love, interrogating,
'Here's a poem, dad; is this a poem?'
Well, it has its place; things
growing, and things dry (another child
clamped on your knee). *What was your question?*

In paddocks, with their rough corners,
the small ghosts of flower or stubble
are husking, the potato-blossoms
of our childhood, the floweret
of the blue-bearded mint: language
of absentee tenants.
There, in the ooze, your audience.
As the wren struts on the rail
you grow land, limestone, Ireland the
animal whose pelt you wear,
into whose brain you echo.

RECOVERY SUITE FOR THOMAS KINSELLA

I

I'd not been there ten minutes
when they told me how sick you'd been,
but nothing else. The start of April.
These were winter quarters
where I sat, boiled crooked by my skin,
and everywhere in Trinity –
the scuffed grass, the rough cobbles,
folly and library, great gates,
heavy doors, lawnsquares and arches –
the fog rose, spitting, as if a plague
spread through your city.
                          No songs
apply to this coincidence. No timeless
chat, no oldtime booze-ups now.

These things make you feel like a loser.
Time to go forward
and touch the edges of our matrix.

II

A whole year the wing of death
snapped at you   and was broken.
Did it remind you of Baudelaire,
'Today for the first time I felt
the wing of madness . . .' (we all know
how it finishes) causing you
to take up glove, scarf, topcoat, go out
strolling, estimating the pavements,
the dandy outsuing death;

and proud, of course, to be alive,
brimming with the effortless stride
of health talk,
greetings and other rhetorics,

pleased with simple configurations, one,
two, three objects on the table,
bread on wooden platter,
heavy outline of book,
something with copper edge turned,
the whole room washed. All
buoyant and quiet as Lascaux.

To which you come in, bustling, from the garden,
not a spark of sweat on you.

III

Simple collocations. The summer pub
at the far side of Phoenix Park,
where the green roils out of the grass-tips at evening,
and where, one evening, we made
our slow decisive entrance, hip and shoulder
to the door, the wooden counter, and the black light
frothing in the glass. Your natal place, almost.

There we sat, unfashionable
as the timber settle, while the midnight
sunset lowered into green water
and the miles of your town, beneath us,
grew lit with their unending lamp
called out by the lamplighter
of the children's voices; and the lights then
echoed back, clear as a voice.

Yet we could see, across them,
the fates of lode and laneway,
phlegmy sidestreets waiting
for false dawn. We saw, we could descry
their myths. Blackpitts, the Coombe,
abrupt turnings past pearl-grey churches,
the pawnbroker's corner,
the canal banks with lumps of wreckage,
and knew it for a myth of burning.

A place that, like Pompeii,
would be remoulded in the burning ash,
a place your people wore
as bridge and covering
to form you this immortal skin.

IV

Cities problematic
as their people. Remember
how under black streets the water-table
lifts and falls; the tides ebb and flow
much as your own skin, moon-curved,
flames and fades, wanes and waxes
to some hidden season; grows thick or thin,
delays, turns scaly,
folds back or splits, until you die
of sheer integument,

your kindred's inbuilt fever.

V

That skin. It puzzled my doctor.
'We know,' he said, 'its natural history.'
But how to cure it? 'Well, it certainly is weird!'
His eyes saw its most intimate lesions;
its red maddened points bulged at his spyglass;
he saw the wonders of that deep
which I conjectured in me,
pushing on me with terror:
the eyelid, so easily
imploded, cognate
with the tight round of the heart,
that artisan muscle, and the soft
pied discolour of the scrotum
that seems painted on,
and the finger webs
and . . .

VI

The day hisses aloud.
Poor poet. Rolled in sweat,
coming (barely alive)
out of the whiskey,
with no strong memory
but poem on poem to add
to what he will never write,
notebook and pen to carry
into the test of night,
and questions to ask: By what
flaw of nature do we grow these
flayed and beaten limbs?

It is the skin punishing us
for what it encloses.
Whiskey or not, we are
landed with our bodies,
earthed there, indeed,
till even muse memory
with its known malicious warmth,
its curled-back tongue,
its inexplicit mobile eyes,
learns how to survive us.

VII

Arrival

They felt, afterwards, at the grid
of the new fire, handling raw meat and oatcake,
they had taken something, a light drift, a virtue,
out of the wave itself; as they cleaned keels
that had gelded the ocean, a fresh eternity
was flexing around them
in the midwater whistling with dolphins,
the trees roughly ranged, whistling in answer.
Then, millenia like a carapace
would roughen out the eyes
to make thin slits of the horizon
burn with cold, and the hands' webs
tingle at the touch of fish dribbling
mercury like a drunk mouth,
the brain teased with memories of how
the cold knife sticks in the flesh.

Then poetry
will be your body's line
to what soul can't remember.

Girl Memory

I remember
how much there was to remember,
the pattern on my blue gloves
the time we built the snow woman.
I remember eating the snow.

The fox with the black stripe crossed
at one point on the path. The owl drifted
over the smooth stone carved
with a woman-shape. Was there
anything else to remember
in that endless line of weathers, like a train
pulling the land behind it?
I remember leaving and arriving:
the car packed like a tin trunk,
everything gently screaming,
and home never arriving

because we were nearly always nearly there.

Revising

Revising the great city poem
in Buswell's; long past midnight;
alert, ears lifted like a hare's
for the tat of faint sounds, in the milky darkness,
nasal spasms up the lightwell,
twists of sub-jazz, sirens
through four streets fading out,
gushes of building sand, cement dust
thick as the steam
in New York roadways,
and cats on the guttering patrolling
eyes down, as if on wire,
you might visualise the brick doorway
of the Passport Office, where the girl
with the huge hessian pack
and empty stomach
lay curled up all morning,
bridling with the cold smell of petrol.

But, dazed with work, you hear
in the next room the woman
gagging with pleasure, on
and on, a smoker's cough of sound.
Molesworth Street three storeys down,
its windows circling like binoculars.

Looking down Thomas Street

Looking down Thomas Street
the house that Jack built,
Sean Gall-hands, son of Gombeen,
Son of Slap-Shoulder,
Son of Sean Geldèr:
Gunmetal the air about them,
house, river and builder.
In that street the butchers were,
and the Butcher's house of prayer;
there, the Pretender's Arms,
there, cathedral worms,
there, the Norsemen's hoard,
there, HQ of An Bord,
there, the tinfeatured streets,
that run all ways from Blackpitts,
plaster and wood torn thin,
the brick with ruined skin,
there, buried in shit and silt,
the house that Jeannot built,
that would not be saved.

The House That

O raw Clanbrassil Street.
A man came and nailed some tin
over the planks
which hid the gaps
that lay in the glass
that broke away from the broken frame
that wet and stank in the crumbled brick
that rose from the town's great shapeless pit
that grew in the house that Jack
made from debris and shit.
This man was a builder. He came
at the word of an absentee
whose ground-rents silently
grew inside the stucco wall
and past the room where the chandelier
was the first thing broken, and the stove
that smelt of piss and gall
and the rats that shrieked beside your ear
and the small twinges of green
that grew on the house he built,
the house he tore and built,
the house we made him build.

Emigrants from Ireland

The Christmas Day emigrants
bound for Kansas City
find that they have to think
more and more about time;
they'd have a drink at the airport
smooth as the waiting plane:
the farewell drink, the Christmas drink,
'When are you home again?'

Maura walking to the plastics factory
in the January rain;
it's better anyway than the ice;
if I had my life again
I'd be off and away to Australia
in a travelling disco-plane.

Working at Dunne's in Patrick St,
queening it over a till,
I see them trudge from shelf to shelf
spending thousands at will.
The lights and fittings creak
as they go out and in;
I take home, regular as sin,
twenty-four notes a week.

Showing Off for the Pipes

The mountain is setting in flame
and he can't take his eyes off
the great plaque of its slope,
a hillside scored for the voice
but made to show off for the pipes

which he takes from the shagreen
bag of suede or broadcloth
in which he carried them, safe
as the pyx and the oils, against floodwater,
or hail, or the heat that untunes them,

which he now allows to sprawl
on his knees, a newborn calf's
flat sides and crossed legs
getting ready to cry. Balanced knife,
one light moved through another,

their waiting and their object
are music; the whole scene is music.
On the hillside the dark falls
and moves about, like a dog
pointing, getting the smells right.

Cambs as a State of Colour

The appleskin colour
hides from the flat sky

and becomes grass. But the road
is edged with the green of cabbage-leaf

and beet dust. If you split open
this county, it would show,
as the beet does, white as coconut;

cattle browse white as hogs,
air white as chemicals
wreathes the bursting towers

so that the black fences, coalboxes,
the tarred roofs of flowersheds,
leave on the cold air
their faint frosty stink.

In their smart cages the canaries
are active as mosquitoes,

the English faces tensely
walking the dog
simper with exasperation.

Nobody here says
'A grand day. Grand.'
certainly no-one
adds, 'Thank God.'

Small Brown Poem for Grania Buckley

Paleface, small fume of fire,
flame that burns nobody,
each time you come into the room
you compose a new colour.

You have mastered the trick
of hovering in doorways
with the fury of the eavesdropper,
peacemaker, magpie at nesting,

Your cardigan worn like an argument,
your runner's legs in straight trousers,
as you stand there, being praised,
as if your whole figure had just been brushed.

Even in the rashness of the close
night, you ask questions about space,
as we watch the black spread like lava
and the stars keep their grip on it
in the pale, pale cold of Kildare.

The neighbours

The neighbours, when I last saw them
in the fur-grey distance down the dried, combed
stubble paddocks, were moving away, slow
as the last smoke of a coal fire,
making you think of the small traces
that have weathered and diverged for aeons
like the microforms of dry watercourses
deep inside shards of dinosaur bones
or knuckles of sequoia fossil.
It was autumn, space of that disorient
time that joins spring to winter,
and the days' ends were turning
abrupt and neat as furrows
or a row of stiches.

Leaving

No matter how hard
I have tried to leave,
walking the distance, back and forth,
three and four times a day,
I can't do it; anyway,
in its own serpentining fashion,
it's left me already:
the green banks finished with me,
the birds winding down out of sight,
the hedgehog, with its delicate
Edwardian dancer's foot
and eyes hunched downward.
Like a weary body, the place
knows when to leave. The place and the body.

Ars medica. The worm-glow
of your entrails on the screen,
the bolt of lightning going
under, like a fish into the sea.

Names

They are dead, and who mentions them
except to point up a joke?
who'd try to save their names
from the hot earth that chokes them?

Like me, they always suffered
the *timor mortis*; but now
I dread, far worse, the black
hole where the eyes vanish

like puckered flesh; and, most,
that careful, numb, soft silence
that sits, while our thoughts lose
body, scale and echo.

Who speaks now of my father
where he is buried without shade,
or who mourns Ian Maxwell
in the hot sun of the pathways?

Who would give one breath
to keep their names in circuit?
Gossip the names of the living,
smudged print the names of the dead.

Theories

I

Those are not selves, but things.
The summer nights begin to float
machine noises weird as kites
over the balconies of the Home Units
in which some transient, motorbike-crazy,
slamming and starting, revs the whole house.

Nor are they symbols. But, dribbling
precious water into the scoops of earth
around the shrubs that burst and die
of sheer scent, you might call them
metaphors, they stick so close to the mind.

To the mind, and to the real.
Most urgently in mid-evening
when, hot still under the fern,
the sparrows cling to the water
and the front garden shines dry as bran.

II

No things but in words
(no Thing but in Word . . .).
Scandalous the leaves rustling
hot and hoarse, not in but against
the lisp of my language:
rolls like a pebble
on the road, stark coming
down with its dogs
all barking, and the man's voice
working set as a ratchet.
Here or in Kildare
that's how the world wags:
No X but in Y.
The roots of language
definite as the wind-cry.

The Too-Lateness
for George Russell

What I hate most
is the too-lateness: when you come
to touch or accept even the smallest
good your life relishes,
you find it slipped
out of its proper time
into some other pace of being,
lost, gone; and you are left dreading
each familiar season, caught
in the mind's alternative society.

And the best, the best, you can
have then, is that freedom
which comes closest, most dear,
when all the best are dead
or dying, or love grown so late
it fastens to you, like a cry
heard decades after,
drilling the sleepless ear,
a child's wail lasting for ever.

Mute freedom of the hospital
or of the sidelines,
the unused time, vacuous with omens
mistaken for sanctity.

Heaven (the name so lovely,
the idea so distant)
lies about us, yes,
but where? From the first light
into which the town
clicks open, and the tussocks
purple like wildflowers, to the last
red tincture in the sunsetting wave.

it moves steady as a clock's
alarming throb, keeping
around us like our own heartbeat;
night jasmine, soft bluebeard mint,
the cool roots of the heat; as you stand
among them, appalled by their completeness,
you'd think heaven the longing for a present
that slips keenly away:
a moment's glow
a figment of the weather.

So Christ, when he outfaced them,
or when he harried his own
with quick asperities: *You know not
the day nor the hour,*
meant: you have not come up to it,
have barely approached it,
or have dreamed past it. Here
I am, I am here,
he taught them: My time a learned time.

There's plenty of time, we said.
There was no time.
The sunny afternoons
were short as blows.

Tomorrows rushed, with less
time to count them
than to drink to their passing.
And that glow in the grass
was where it all started,
cold, with the unearthly
blood-chill of the salt life-forms,
sucked into walls porous as limestone,
to stay there, like a leaf-fossil
mimicking eternity:

the Oldest Animals.
And you and I go on, mazed
in the Byzantine closed mesh of nature
when all we wanted
was some place in a story.

Narrative

Why do we tell stories
so brazenly about ourselves?
She sits in the half-rocked chair
as if swung between bells
wondering about remembering.
Folie de grand-mère.
He holds the steering-wheel
as if shaking the car, whose tension
thus forces him to lean backward
like a retired handyman.
Any moment he will be clouted
by the young woman in the too-edgy Volvo
who pauses, strokes her hair,
then smells her straightened fingers.
She is pushing herself out of narrative
because no-one, certainly not I,
can make her credible.
What story is she in?
This child will never step from the kerb,
this woman never stop walking
with her Safeway bags and grey coat
round and round the sun-shadowed streets.
They are all balancing. I am preparing
(them?) myself for some arcanum
in my own story.

Conversations

Monday mornings cleaning the folders,
Thursdays re-editing our dead,
the evenings converting fear into boredom,
drawing up the tight strings of past time.
The old, I write, are a class of triumphs
towards which we conspire; my one ambition,
I murmur, is to grow old. Eventually.
And healthy. Think of it, a healthy old man.
Yesterday I said to my friend the poet,
Those people over there are listening
as if you were a politician,
a wise woman, a gypsy, or
chief elder of the tribe: as if
touching you might bring luck.
Good luck or bad? he asked.
But don't mind that. They are composing something.
And, composition is mostly listening
said the young musician
through his melancholy cigarette.

Love

Casually love
accepts its blindness,
pats its dull favourite on the head
saying 'You've never seen a clumsier
clot than this one'; and nags the others
'Come on. Are you going to be all night?'
Casually we pass into summer,
season of police-sirens, amplified rock,
a crush of laughs from balconies.
Love chooses a dirndl
and browns itself from toe to buttock,
from crotch to eyebrow,
presuming on time's favouritism.

Sheer Warmth

The lost opportunities
began at the hearth-side
that almost from infancy seduced us
with a rectangle of heat, saucepans, black kettle,
the bricks breathing slowly a film of ash,
and the banked glow of woodcoals
at the back, against the iron ploughshare.
Our ghosts come in near it, and begin
again the time lost in warmth; the pen
stuck down the spine of *David Copperfield*
won't be used that night, and poems
gone missing in a dream
won't last beyond the shins' stiffening.
This is sheer warmth, porous as limestone.

A writing life started in that room
and rooms like it. We learned delay there,
indulged the dread of finishing
and going on. Now weekends frighten me.
Sunday. The rains have come, sweeping
a chisel's edge to the northwest corner
and the trees bud and bend in their flashes.
We have built right above the burning
shifting earth's core, so that the gardens
glow as if founded on volcanoes,
and all your lines recall your child-heat,
its level rooms, its share of sickness.

A Tincture of Budapest

I have lived for thirty years
with a tincture of Budapest,
the reddish hills of Buda, whose long bridges
filled squares with the living, then with the dead,
the burning factories caught in the water,
the brown bodies held fast

in their skin, in a photograph
of almost winter. I learned Csépél,
Kilian, to set beside Kossuth,
and saw the plumbing of war stretched across
Petöfi Square, Bem Square, Republic Square,
with the gun barrels burnt at their corners.

I learned the unconscious of maps
in those photos; their waters broke in my dreams
of a city wound on to a river
like a great fabric on a spool. I learned Györ,
Pecs, the call signs of free radios,
I learned borders, entries and exits.

I learned that no killings give me pleasure;
the AVO grouped by the wall for execution
lean together, their eyes squeezed so thin
it looks as if the wind blows their faces.
Next they are seen sprawling on the ground.
Next, it is said, laughing at café tables.

The camera is deadlier than the gun.
The freedom fighters in their long thin coats and armbands
fell too. They lay crushed like flags
on the buckled tram lines. There time will drench them
and the text books will make them faint and drab,
and only the poet as historian will discern them.

And yet how useless poets are, how feeble
their anecdotes and promises.
History leaves them staring resentfully
as cities they'd farewelled, now long rebuilt.
If they are needed it's only as a town
needs bells; or as a bell needs echoes.

It's just that each of us has a lost language,
to be cherished and built back,
piece by piece, into the mind.
Like Cornish. Kernow. Whose very name
became its myth, so that it can't be spoken
without a spine chill. Mine is Hungary.

Deathmares

Summer nights are the worst. Deathmares
pull the staring body
stiffly from bed
to grope against eerie and insecure
interiors: panels of ship, plane, or coffin,

fabrics, winding-sheets, rough sides of hessian.
No space to pause or turn in,
no presence that will hear you,
no blinds to raise on the blackness
glimmering outside, in street and garden.
But the pain of a scraped wrist
is almost enough
to free that catatonic self
drifting in the dream-triangle.

Or some other, monitoring self
brings back for you
the processions that we once walked in
with white shirts, with red sashes
our mothers pinned at our shoulders;
long swept away like damp leaves,
their colours absorbed in the pavements

where I wrestle to understand
how, even in the pit, we expect dreams
to contain protectors.

Trumpet Voluntary

Wind wave, hurry after, land rush; and the distant surf
heaves it up further, till the house is hissing,
the cliffs breaking like hurdles, the well-bronzed echo,
as you walk in the consensuality of a moment
you are lifted between the legs by a gale force
strong as the blood of your youth.

Now that you can feel old age
becoming a habit, like a migraine,
take to walking in the garden in the cool of morning,
regressing steadily towards the marvellous
and looking out to the salt shine where the trawlers
count those straits and capes, those gulping reefs
that lead us on, outward, past the islands
licked with light, the hasty and tough marram,
whatever is oceanic, spare and bounteous,
composing the home that won't surrender us.

You'll go out quiet as the suck of the tide,
not at all mothy and warm; but the ground's air
is so filled with delicate moistness, you may say
I have begun to breathe dew; that is the accomplishment
of my dying; that is my death-skill; and looking up
you hear the islands soon inhale your future.

An Easy Death

Death makes its sweep over the grass,
wind rolled in leaves, a torn wing.
An answering fickle beat
flaps at the ribcage.
Get rid of these cups and saucers,
the transistor, the pattern-rugs,
this dull heap of necessities
I saved up for once. Recycle the poems,
clean off the margins of these books,
give them back to the poor
from whom they came.

Heart jerks in its black triangle.
It's too hot for change, too late
for wills and testaments,
too dark for growing up
into the strain of the new life.

If I could go blank
as the crow's picked bones,
or burn out, quick as pine branches,
and be finished with it,
men and women,
friends, the work half-marshalled,
the squalor of deprived places,
the flayed and reeking countries,
and care for nothing
but the sun on this brass ring,
those dead breast bones.

But I've been down so deep
there's no strength to wish
anything, even that blankness;
I have let go;
already
I am falling from their picture.

Catholics, we were trained for it,
the maze of words, the candles
unrolled from years of tissue paper
for this moment, the petite firm
forward-leaning priestly movements,
necessary as the dying itself;
trained to compose the soul
for all crises: death, cancer, waste of summer,
insolence, neglect, humiliation,
the drying-out of friends,
the uncouth stroke of money,
the ordeal of home-going,
the rising mist of time,
this priest packing his cold oils.

And Thomas Hardy, dour optimist,
thought they would all be thinking of him
at that moment, murmuring like leaves
about the leaf of his passing,
quiet strong people communing, 'He was a man
who used to notice such things.'

But think of your name as something
burnt up in a moth-flight,
thrown off by a self which has learned
to seize its oblivion
for the sake of memory.

Memory: the hinge

Memory: the hinge
on the closing door,
the flapping smells
subversive as brothers,
re-working your attention,
                      So
the butterfly stopped
phone died in the air
your throat rose, stark open,
as if you meant to speak
into melting heat,
Trees running in the air,
back and forward, stayed
like herons on a frieze
And jasmine at my back, jasmine
that swayed loose, gave
power to the sunset breeze.

Down Scannell Lane

Down Scannell Lane the bats
looped in the nightfall's strawberry colour
and made you walk through them
into a tunnel's gleam of darkness.
Was it that sight you recalled,
or the preternatural sound, or the smell
of brussels sprouts packed in boxes
tight as books in a library, smelling
of woodworm, or claps of dust?

In Waterbeach, Ely was outworld;
they knew nor king nor Cromwell;
it was the Baptists came here, scything,
at the mid-century harvesting;
and all my neighbours' voices,
tilting the ends of sentences,
upcraking like a pheasant's
with its starter-motor suddenness,

spoke Baptist: a whole dialect of the sinus.
Miss Crout, Mr Sowden, Mrs Pink,
came they by laneway,
by bridge or by causeway,
met at the Co-op door
and, as their voices dipped and floated,
stayed safe inside their vowels,
however much they dripped
with gathered moisture,
with smells of wood in wet earth.

Waterbeach

There was no need for talk.
The bye-path ran into the mash of fields
unsteadily as string. It was not the dead
you'd fear in this closure.
It was the sluggish living frightened us
As evening fell, you'd see
edged into that system scarecrows
leaving their centre, running
the cabbage-ruffs were black dreap shadows
the damp and the smell crept together
spread and clamped down, strong as a hand
till they reached the earth under the stone
Night grew its slugs of frost
all night the flats rang with breath
at 7 of the morning they was
trudging again up the bye-path, men
with spade and mattock, hawking and spitting
not needing to talk.

Telephone, old friend,
why didn't you tell me we were drunk
the night you rang, and we both heard
nothing but breathing?

BOOZE YEARS

I

Six or eight booze years,
as I may as well call them,
stay in the memory
with a smell like creosote,
a deep hospital smell
that no showers could wash entirely
from your rubberized flesh.
On a hot morning it walked with you
into headlights of the sun.

It could be a picture by Brueghel,
Death and the social drinkers,
each of whom, in the group,
is dreaming dizzily of love,
nothing particular, but things
arranged as in the old days,
a warmth as general as daylight
waiting for 'I still want you',
terrified of hearing 'I need you'.

Private pains and scandals
Grew to argument in a buzz of newness.
'Isn't there some badge you could wear?'
I asked them, 'Something that says
You are on the side of history
or, simply, born to win?'
But they said No; they were concerned persons.
One said, 'I guess I'm an idealist.'

Think how the nights ended
the nights of friendship and defeat,
the gramophone pounding out Irish,
on the table empty glasses
pushed out to look neat and helpless,
and yourself, or someone, talking, talking.

II

In Our Youth

Being athletes, we never touched it.
If there were vital fluids
for the body to keep intact,
booze would never be allowed to taint them.

You could locate virtue in muscle-tone,
in the sprung rhythm of a way
of walking, looking proudly around,
ready to sprint to the rescue.

It was certainly not leaning in pubs,
grazing the bar counter,
or swopping fools' laughter.
It was in keenness. Keenness.

III

After a Layoff

Coming back to it after a layoff
you tremble a bit, your gut kicks,
Christ, what if you're not wanted?
But it comes warm, like the squeeze of a woman,
as if to say, good luck, it's been a long time,
but you're always welcome, no problems.
And as the heat reaches the pit of your stomach
you feel filaments lit up with relief,
with freedom, the new self-possession
of one who has recovered his nerves and muscles.
I have to tell you,
down the years of crossed wires,
Whiskey, O Whiskey, you are no mere tempter,
You are like the start of a race or a poem
running, and not bitching about finishing.

But wouldn't you be pleased

But wouldn't you be pleased if the war ended?
Bill Collins kept asking. I said Of course;
But P. M. wouldn't say the words.
That was a hangover morning, a sunlit morning
In a Grade A booze year. I stood upright for work
As if to haul the Flag. I concentrated
(Who is this in the corner, concentrating
so that the world may not go unredeemed?)
I lived in a room, with the sound of fifes,
The smell of kerosene, a smooth brown light.
I travelled to another room every day
And taught them what I could. Then drank.
Or sat and listened. I was listening
All the time. The classes came and went
With the easy ranting of cicadas. No, not happy.
But putting the materials together.

SYDNEY VISIT

Northern Prospect

You forget the rictus of envy
and the three (or four) born winners,
and the glitter of culture-money
and the poets fighting in lifts
while the cliff caves hide the stone snakeheads
and the salt moon floats on Warrawee.

Even in these dun green suburbs
where, padding from drink to drink in thongs,
they don't notice their own flame-trees,
you are setting foot on blessed soil;

Sydney winding Sydney
lying in its own arms,
estuary, steep road, bushland,
seed of water and jacaranda,
the mynahs cracking the green boughs

the long mothering gullet
that fed them once, and suffers
the gross repeating appetites.

And, lifted everywhere onto heights,
you see this city best in the flash of an echo
where the wingtip rolls on Clovelly
and the mountain sets longingly over the harbour
and you want to go down again
to the waterface breaking into mirrors;
all Sydney, then, breaks through sunlight
to let the ferries slow down
for Cremorne Point, for Manly, for the whole Pacific.

I'll be there next month,
Warrawee swooping with redwinged birds,
not a cloud on the earth
or in the sweating heaven.

Eastern Prospect

The harbour breaks up in thunders of sunlight
that is suddenly a Loch Ness presence
under the piers; and the Moreton Bays
push up their Romanesque humps, from roots as deep

as Western Civilisation (which was heard falling
flake by flake, all through the recent summer);
but it keeps up, festooned with the old tabus,
although an ocean wind is biting at it.

All intimately foreign: the straw boaters
and pob-faced uniforms on Strathfield platform,
sunblazed roofs of cars creeping down
endlessly from Parramatta; and the *plein air*

stairways, open foliage, stone shoulders,
(*le tout l'esprit d'escalier*), the horizontal
frames of a city vertical as any
you can think of, radiating on white sand.

Who in the tempest will save the Sangster mansion?
Who will stand by Kirribilli House
with his swaggerstick, crying Back, get back there,
as if the angels of war were just a mob

Of Indonesians milling in his courtyard?
Who will go bail for the children of the sewers
or plant the stones like figs again? Slowed down,
the ferries stick, bee-like, in the oil of sunset.

Life Style

Rounding home at midnight
with a metal clash of doors, handrails,
lights thrust on, Bunty swearing
at the grit streaks through her hair:
Play hard and, by God,
travel hard. And that's the way you'd like

the neighbours to remember you.

Next morning, smart in a jacket that
never went anywhere near the beach,
Keith, Roger strides out with the briefcase
and the colourful striped tie: the kids to school,
lunch with a pair of after shaves,
Look mister, work hard, life's
not all four wheel drives and beach houses

whatever the bloody neighbours think.

Getting Away

The mangroves on your left cool and sunken,
drive into the sun's moving flare-path
that throws off its wheels of glitter
and hooks and retrieves them
like platens from the water,

thinking of Camden and the cool plains.

HOSPITAL SUMMER, WESTERN SUBURBS

Concord Infirmary

I was down to Concord Infirmary
and I saw the Matron there,
her cheeks were warm as a postcard girl's
and a starched veil on her hair.

She called out jokes to the sickies
humming 'Don't Make Me Cry',
and she ran No. 2 Infirmary
with a wild gleam in her eye.

The old hands said, She's a beauty,
dinkum, a heart of gold;
but I knew she was just passing the time
with geezers in from the cold.

And she'll leave Concord Infirmary
stepping out with her officer boy,
her captain, who'll be calling tonight
to cash in on his bundle of joy.

Let her go, let her go, God bless her,
with her sentimental airs,
imitating the Andrews Sisters
or the hipswinging Squadronaires.

There were forty men in the cardiac ward
steamy as a bloody tent.
The matron's pet name was Glenda,
and she loved winning an argument.

I did time in Concord Infirmary,
and I lost my seedtime there,
stretched out on my back on a Government bed
so drab, so thin, so spare.

Western Prospect

Not for tribute, but to pay old debts,
not from nostalgia, but for simple
tesserae of love, once laid down
in mean quarters, and recalled now
in colours unburdening the mind.
It was in the war I came here
for the first time, idiotic as a boy, in love with
the barbed lightness of his nature,
brought here, brooding like an electric current
over my body's not-doing.
I could not be messenger or hero.
I could not drive, could barely walk.
With my eyes closed, I imitated
the soft mimesis of the sea
flooding into brightness at the Heads.
Prostrate, my blood thick with acids,
I sent my mind out like a curved beak,
my thoughts out active as a brood of wheat birds.
In the late afternoon, suddenly
there would be cotton uniform dresses
breathing health into my eyes.
She would walk the length of the ward
carrying her uniform hat
down by her side. Her hair was brushed
to gleam like the horizon. Sit down beside
my bed, my wireless big as a Coolgardie,
'Hullo. What aria is it this time?'
By overwhelming majority decision
the world famous tenors sang behind us,
leaving their bruit upon the air.
No other arias, no late love songs.
But I felt a man. I felt young.
I felt a young man,
not something to be rolled in sheets
for cleaning and injecting.
It's years since I remembered her.
But every friendship
needs to be called love,
and every love
deserves an elegy.

Landlocked

It was like the mockup of a suburb,
and you were inside it
almost mute, totally indoors;
except for glimpses of duckboards
and the ends of walkways.

There I lasted into summer,
hospital summer, in the western suburbs,
fans caught in the air
like flies in a spider web,
a tree stiff with heat at the corner,
and the wireless playing 'Paper Doll'
while the hearts of the new arrivals
went thrum, thrum, tharrumm,
all through the dark night
of the soul, and the anarchic organs.

You heard the wind, but saw no branches,
you saw sun-bleach on the windowsills
but no sun climbing or delaying;
your speech was all of yes, yes, and no, no,
you met the tours of inspection every day;
you nodded like a toy, you leaned back on the bedrail,
getting better, being cured, endlessly,
they told you with careful eyes.
Someone had lent you photographs of Manly.
That was 113th AGH, Concord,
not seed but cutting time,
thin whiplike branches cut from the red hibiscus,
seasons cut from your life,
blood cut from the heartbeat.

None of us learned understanding
or got wisdom.
And the great shade is fallen about us,
striplings and old soldiers,

young crocks and old hopefuls,
all, in the middle of our journey,
relieved to be bossed by women.

For we have no landscape outside or inside us;
the heart limps round its territory;
put somewhere, but not placed anywhere,
we have no answers
for one another's questions
except the fumbles of our pasts.

If I had known
how close we were to water,
the brackish, the flowing, the breeze-caught,
how that breeze came from Yaralla Bay,
those cool airs and swirls of rain
from Rocky Point and Kissing Point,
that faint musk from the bends of river,
I would have sent my soul out
like a sightseer on a wharf
to look for hours across the water,
to query and consult tides,
the light inside them red as resin.
But so far as I knew we were landlocked.

The wise healers nodded, and I nodded,
the handmaidens smiled, O do smile,
show you are grateful, O *be* grateful.
I nodded, stiffly, like a toy.

Nervy city

Nervy city: caverns pouring out talkers
at St James or Museum
straight into the shade of trees;
thoughts walking the street whiz in
and out of your head, like a dazzle of figleaves.
From one upstairs bar to another
you breathe this speckled beer,
no sooner drunk than sweated out.
Always have a full middy on hand,
Said the eminent journalist. So I tried.

And I heard more scandal
than anybody could take in.

The truth is, I forgot them,
too many of them, profiles I once roomed with,
voices I learned like light patterns,
people from whom I took, to whom I gave
time, in segments, to share like an orange.
While Murph hammed it up for his family
after Mass, at Bondi, the sea flexed around me
through gaps and entries between the buildings.
To hell with Murph. I forgot the rugby,
and the Newcastle gallops, and the snaps
the girls would send, on the least provocation.
I forgot, forever, sergeants and corporals,
and all the officers I hadn't even noticed.
I knew the sea had a use,
but I'd not yet found it.

I've forgotten the names

I've forgotten the names, or mislaid them
to gather dust like heads on pillows
in Concord, or Manly, in grass by the long rivers,
in Glebe, in the deserted sunlight.

I've even forgotten the people,
their dryness and coolness
in those humid wards and bar-rooms,
their touch, soft as a feather on the jawline,
hot glaring Sydney.
Stay here, they were saying; why do you have to go
    home?
I forget what I said; I remember
evening swam crimson on the ceiling;
I found myself talking to them
as if they were strangers, or tourists,
of flame-trees or poincianas,
and colour, I told them,
the soul of everything,
rhythm the soul of everything.

The Tuning-Time

I would not call it night
it was the height of evening,
Schwarzkopf singing from the Town Hall stage,
and with the wineglass in your hand
there was nor youth nor age
but Summer, bridling down the avenues.

I'd never call it morning
it was the throat of noon,
McEwan singing High Mass in St Pats,
and as the choir went thudding past
you sang too: youth nor age
but Summer brimmed up through the weighty cool.

I dare not call it pride
it was the tuning-time,
the lucky nights when Jussi Björling sang
bel canto through the garden scent,
a time not youth nor age
but well-groomed Summer glistening like hair.

Old Jazz Persons

Played on the burning Corso,
played for the perfect Australian sand,
played the breezes on the hotel flags,
the flapping colours, and the chords drifting
in and out of Fisherman's Stomp,
and out of Pharaoh's Rag.

Jazz players old with youth.

And the fifty-year-old jazzmen,
pretending forty-five,
rose up into the heat, and played
riffing like demons. Sweat
ran into their eyes and hair,
and they lifted their sounding profiles.
The grids of the past are here,
I bring out old photographs,
play all the sharp dead faces,
play the brilliantine hair,
play us jiving in the dancehall,
and the girls with their well-trained calves
knocking us back all year.

Brunny Town Hall

Dancing in the jazz hall at the Brunny Town Hall,
with a girl that Eddie fancied, doing a line for him,
I said, my mate's shy (much as to say,
And I'm representing him)
'And you're not, I suppose.'
Oh yes, I'm shy as anything,
but I was keen to have this dance.
So we hit the waxed fresh dance-floor
and slid on the rosined boards
and she held my hand against her back
as I murmured close to her ear,
'I'll dance with you in the greenwood'
and she said, 'He's a bloody ratbag,
but he sure can dance.'
As you swung them into corners
they'd be sniffing your breath for beer
and they'd be humming song after song.
In the country's crisis
that was the war's worst year.

Three days to the loss of summer

Three days to the loss of summer,
and when will you be gone, yourself?
With one suitcase, to the turn in the road,
to the mailbus, and the oldfashioned junction,
the train from Bendigo, the stacks of ships,
and things I won't let myself imagine.

How many years till I see you coming
grownup and welldressed, up the new road,
like a civil servant making a visit?
And the lights will have set like flaws in the glass.

A man, a woman

A man, a woman, straighten up from where
they have been dragged by a kerosene tin
they cooked and did their washing in. Their shoulders
are bent and lifted by it. Now, on the fire,
it makes a yellowish steam spitting round
its rim and sides: the cauldron of the poor.

Yet they burned good fuel, pinecones,
mallee roots, messmate and resin wood.
They raked twigs and stalks to catch the fire.
They sat round telling Depression jokes
of pannikin bosses, flash clobber, and winning Tatts.
Memory is unreliable and self-serving,
as the critic said. But I recall the flame-core,
the cores of all the flames, as vivid yellow
turning to vivid orange, like cordial in the water,
like the new gush of petrol in the old puddle,
like meaning in a quarrel. I won't forget that.

Oral History

My grandfather farming the sour land near the creek
(you might as well be ploughing a salt lick)
and Ned Kelly's father up from the bark hut
at Beveridge, for a Kilmore christening,
a wake, or a burial, one of those Catholic rorts,
met, perhaps, in the Red Lion. Four or five of them,
'Well, how's it goin, Red, are yeh making a living?'
'Not much of a living anywhere round here.
But you've got to keep goin. There's the kids to think of.'
(Ned Kelly, and my uncles; in a few years, my father –
the kids there was to think of). Red Kelly drives
back inside his hut with the northern woman
he always dreaded leaving. And Patrick Buckley,
the silky little dynast, bronze age farmer,
back to the scrub and to his wife's plantbeds.
By God, it was lonely pioneering Springfield,
and Beveridge ripped at the soul like wilderness.

In comes the gentle critic we love so much,
'Well, it's good to see someone writing of ordinary people.
What? Ned Kelly's father and my grandfather?
Ordinary people my arse. They were chained foxes.

Introvert as Horseman

The introvert as horseman.
Staring as if at your relations,
See him there
in sepia, hat cocked, leggings
tight as a Nazi's, and you can
place him, any way you like, a black stump,
for example, on the creek-bank,
the stick in his right fist
tapping at nothing,
the soil ghostlike as steam,
or full of nostalgia in the kitchen
keeping an eye out for
the last century, the century of lost marriages.

The money in the bank, the suits,
the pony-and-trap, the watch-and-watchchain,
the silver-dented sets of harness,
proxies for the land; and so were
the brick house he had almost started to build
for his bride-to-be
that nobody had met; and the smoke-browned portrait
of his mother swaddled to the neck.
He noticed these; but he kept love
for the great purebred shire horses,
with their plumed feet stamping, and their shoulders
rubbing the trees, the old blind one,
Sailor, still serving
his droves of mares in the dustbowl,
the sweat drops thick as wool scrapings
on the fence, the lintel brown with mugginess,
the crooked iron tanks, the ungrowing light.

Seabreeze

Houses made them, square frames
that drew themselves up, and spread out
until they could be felt as homes.
Yours had the glassed-in verandah
and white corners guarded by pinetrees;
it was always calm, spic and spanned
by the climate, so it appeared, like old resin.
Brother and sister, there you grew
into your self-conscious thirties,
styled like characters in a book.

Straightbacked woman, you
became the paleness of the summer, riding
with your English rose-tempered skin
delicately through the clods of dust
between cowpats and thistles,
would come on no audience
but one small startled boy. And he
would look up from his book
to see a book-character coming on,
riding steadily, the saddle gripped with spruce knees.

How did you bear the heat
in your cool jodhpurs? We
were local as the creekbeds,
we were heat-experts,
we breathed it like dew
even on scorching days, when moonlight
stifled in our darkened rooms, and air
had not yet been invented, seabreezes,
however marvellous, stayed near the sea.

Your brother, into town for the bank
or the stock and station agent,
stepping in cavalry twill
from his *déclassé* tourer,
looked nobody in the eye.

Remember, if you are still alive
(a soft-cheeked seventy-five),
the grapes without name or flavour,
the hoppers in the grass crackling
like cicadas, the parched bull-calves,
the paddocks filled with hides rotting,
yourself riding out the summer.

I hope you are safe in some city
where the seabreezes come frivolling
up the bay's crescent
to service air and conversation,
and are walking on some high verandah.

We knew that the sea was heaven

We knew that the sea was heaven,
but we had never seen it.
We dwelt miles away in limbo,
all summer an incompetent fury
thinned our mouths, hardened our skin,
made us unable to imagine
those blue echoes in the shelly water
that pulled back over the sand. We could not
imagine heaven, either, but knew
it would be-cool,
gutted of heat, with air-shafts moving
into breezes fresh with mud and seaweed.

Of course, through childhood, stories
would circulate of the bliss of water.
We let them ripen as we would
any High Gossip, like furtive talk
of sex or female bleeding. As with
God, we attached ourselves warmly
to each story, while believing none.
No scapulars could guarantee water.
No prayers brought the rivers closer.

Each January the creek dried,
and we saw the willows' rotted base
pushing back the earth. The paddocks
were scored with everything (of wood,
or skull-bone, or leather) everything the sun
bent, twisted and preserved
till the dead grass disappeared beneath it.

Summer was like learning Latin,
something to look back on,
to murmur like a tune.

Often the plate held black trout

Often the plate held black trout or redfin,
smooth-brown sections of eel,
or other tough natives of narrow waters;
but, red or pale, salmon came from the tin.

We were aliens to the deep world.
A small waterfall, yes, in the spiny bush,
flat lagoons, a threadlike creek in flood,
a swamp heavy as the Mississippi,

but no sea could materialise among
the hairy lengths of cut timber
in the sawmill or the school built from it,
among the giant ferns or ant-hills.

These have put dryness everywhere,
they made you climb for your pleasure,
they showed you no pulse in the hills,
they were as much despair as you could take.

Deep of Evening
for Tim Kelly

You see the children
running in their loose ellipses;
they touch base, rise and fall,
nerves planned like animals;
branches touched by the pane,
spokes brightening in the wheel.

You have polished and arranged,
set the day straight for hours,
and now you can appear to let time happen
as your ear waits uneasily
on the house shifting, or the cat-squeal
of a nail in timber. Night coming.
Patience is a brand of courage.

What we wait for is the cool change,
the Cool. The small towns'
version of the Spirit, their sweating on it
a service of the mystery.
For someone born in hot places
the main thing is to last,
to come loping
up long vistas like the young cricketer
you still seem: the soul
still pushing forward, leaf by leaf,
walking upright. In whatever season.

Now at midsummer, filaments
glow, in the light dusk, cayenne red;
we have cooled down into thunder;
and the rain comes, light rain, the bowl of
the hills washed with lightning,
the water's moss smell, the trees
agleam like wires
in sunset swelling with its light clicks
of humid air; each node
of matter loosening
in the wet cheeping silence,
the deep of evening.

Brothers

Once we were close
as the dark jerseys
pegged on the clothesline, touching
and crossing,

while birds struck at the budding apples
and heavy scales
grew inch by inch
along the cherry branches.

Close again now. Last night
I dreamed the curving sloped road
that takes you into Romsey,
and the white, strained bridge
and the house

where in the large sagging bed
we rolled, jeering at each other
with that cubbish landlocked, fratricidal
hatred of the Summer,
the dour heat splashing down like rain,
hitting and squealing, 'Stop
mocking me. I hate you. Stop
bloody bloody mocking . . .'

moon low and thin on the verandah's
dusty gleam, and the old hawthorn
whitening like a crown of thorn.

Brothers, doppelgängers, we
paused in our fighting as the shadows
of its bare crackling boughs began
to rush in and out of windows
as if mirrors ebbed and flowed
the night away. The dawn would show us

pent, splayed like spiders
in our dried sleep,
the air coated with dust,
the curtain stuck to the sill.

Outside a world where
everything was curved, and leaf and bough
seen through the bend of water.

Lights glint on dust

Lights glint on dust. On tussocks.
On car bonnets. On a small walking face.
He takes the note, wanders
diagonally down Main Street,
gawking, stupid as a leaf,
his eyes all hair and cheekbones,
believing in the world
that bears him up. That will go soon.
Even as he goes his messages.

BROUGHT UP ON THE FEARS OF WOMEN

I have many terrible
pictures in me.
They are all of women:
of women leaving
or promising, and not coming back,
scattering their hair like leaves,
and their smell like the earth-smell.

That was last night's dream

They fell and were falling
I stretched out my hand to save them
and I was falling. The smell
of jasmine followed me like grit
into the Venetian light of morning.

You are such a bad dreamer,
you retain only a scene brown as varnish
and there, in the foreground,
a version of yourself, feigning memory
to arrange the slats of the story.

In that sleepmind where
they lie too close to each other,
the fibrillating words
torture the dream-images, printing
postcards of identity

The small girl hopped
and stood, waiting,
Bert and Clive Brown jerked at her dress
their hands shoved under it
she moved back, off balance,
they pulled at her knickers.
The boy stood at the gap in the palings
and felt that strange stiffening
that pushed out his dick

[141]

In the sleepmind what
is that small roundfaced boy
doing? He is listening,
he is watching, touching the palings,
beginning the stiffness of fear and pity,
turning clumsily away
flatfooted along the betrayed fence,
picture, self, words
kept in his soul for later.
Also, he is doing nothing.

How do they see themselves?
Provoking. Being admired.

When do they live most magnetically?
Combing one another's hair.

In front of what audience?
A man. A group of peers. A mother.

How high do their eyes go?
Higher than the shriek of bats.

O quick hands, gloves, partitioned hair,
O futures burnt out in the air,

Mimics of rust, they did not make you wise,
the tilted hat, the soft observant eyes,

the straight seat on a horse, the dancing-floor
that spun you breathless laughing hour by hour,

they did not save you; neither did your choice
of last defence, the glove and supple voice.

You grow old, your fingers weaker than
bones of a discarded fan.

[142]

Brought up on the fears of women,
we could not wait to grow families
of our own; we grew them
arrogantly, as you might plant
the nerve system of a garden
or fix mannerisms in brick walls,
high cypress mazes, mansions, *cultures*,
in which we read the great Viennese
who created us. We could not wait
to give our fearfulness a home.

The Table

The table is set,
the grandees in their places.
Could you tell from how they eat
the lie of their faces?

Time, said Beckett, will tell
with whatever tact it has,
with the deft thunder of the clock's bell;
time, ending itself, will end it.

And if the book was published
at the right moment,
and whether it was received unjustly,
or whether it caused torment,

or whether the poet was silent
for what remained of his life,
none of this matters at all;
it fades on the edge of the knife.

the joy we have had will quiver
to light again over the poems
we can no longer write; eyes give,
receive, a kaleidoscope of forms.

Bring in the fashionable painter
to preserve it all,
the table set in its oval,
girded by full-bodied diners,
the tapestry on the wall
with its wildeyed hunting scene.

Seeing Romsey

I see Romsey through a hole in the wind
as I used to in late autumn, in the southern gales,
just there, not vibrating with changes
but like a model that has grown to its full height.
The timber houses have roofs of painted iron,
the brick ones are lowering with warm tiles.
The tree near me is the one I climbed
fifty-three years ago. I smell *roses* on the fence
where once the whole air was brushed with cypress.
Proust's madeleine, nothing. Even the smell
of trains that haven't run here
for forty years. Smelling strong as they slow down.
Smell of the comics they brought each Saturday.
Proust's madeleine was nothing to this,
or Eliot's hyacinths and lilacs
or that great heap of blossom in Yeats's window.
Nothing to this. To the firesmell of the forge,
squeezing into the smell of burning hoof. Incense
through the voices singing *O Salutaris hostia*
that never sing Latin any more.
I smell the printer's ink, and books,
and dust that flashes when the raindrops hit it
as it takes the rain into itself.

The Child is Revenant to the Man

In the frayed apple leaves a grin of copper.
The figtree tied its arms together
Just as you were learning to be one thing
You were forced to become another;

You saw the horizons change size,
you gritted your mind and mourned
their grey, crimson, their sisterly blue.
Many dreams lay down in those fringes.

Before your lust started you could see
there would be no-one to receive it fully:
You, the anonymous you
of modern poems, to whom daythings happen,

You are in your proper time, it is I,
the I which is so filled with dread
I almost welcome nightmares, who have
slipped out of it

and see time as that endless past in which
I am getting ready, I am almost ready
to play my part in the colourful, nuanced
contradictions of sky and figtree.

A Poetry Without Attitudes

A poetry without attitudes

that, like a chance at happiness,
arrives too late, so candid
it will seem secret
and will satisfy no-one,

be useless in seminars
and will certainly aggravate critics

and force even the publisher
to speak of a New, a Mature voice

while actually you are learning
to walk with it, to lie against it,

your earth-tremor, your vibrato
turning you slowly into song.

The Watch's Wheel – Pieces and Songs

A longing for what you have been reading,
a longing for what you heard
just now, for what you will taste tomorrow
Looking into the live moment,
into the shine of the watch's wheel

These in Their Wet Darkness

You are like those who cheer armies
and weep for rich people lost in landslides.
These are a people no-one has seen in public,
ancient as lampreys in their wet darkness.

Maps

The country has sunk into its maps
and lives a new range of colour
from faint brush green to faded rust;
the hills look like a tank-trap,
the rivers appear and disappear
like a child's drawing of an eel.
It sinks deeper, into books
that clasp and close it in, a texture
that holds it to the printed page.

The invader sees it there, and turns
it inside out for shapes.
Armies, glitters of silverfish,
drain at every indentation,
suck at the sea-furrows

from language to consciousness.

The South Side of Dublin

At dusk the sluttish children
Wandered down the Grand Canal
Where the soft lights lean over dark.
Who'll catch them when they fall?
The deep soft-red punished brick
Called their voices in
And wall and sky grew close together
Down the south side of Dublin.

The broken jaws of Camden Street
Ash blackening the Coombe
You'd never need the Liberties
To give your body room

In Kevin street the pelting shadows
Turned their heads to grin
The dusty men and widows mourning
Out the south side of Dublin.

In Coombe and Clanbrassil
you'll walk the rocks of bawn
A grit like fire, a wind that blows
The sand out of the stone
The ratlike birds in Leeson Street
The sky grained like a skin
And sweat drains off the aimless body
In the South side of Dublin.

Castle Bees

October's clutch of warm days
moistens the flowerheads again
so they wrinkle, and make their thudding movement
into the air whose dry
crop-colour's gone into the great
flushes of mushroom-white
that transform sky and stone walls.
So thick a morning it draws the bees
from their bowslit, so they go
a controlled tongue pouring upwards
to the next stone fissure:
a rage for mobility
and brief anguish.

The two cars at an angle, ticking,
are just off for the midlands
leaving behind us these green creepers
that look stuck to the walls
with a light white as glue, and the unmonitored
bees climbing back, up and down
through their body-sounds. Sparks
hissing up as if on velvet,
plovers reaping the midland reedbeds.

'I have tried
to imagine the Irish before the Sadness,
and I can't. It is like a change
dividing the sea-creatures
from their land-shapes. And yet
it seems to me a rational sadness.'
Above the pink-wet stones of Burren
raven and peregrine drift slowly,
stone world, cold swimmers
casting the shadow of a fish.

Fine Western Land

I

Born landlocked, as we were,
sunk all our childhood
in the biggest island,
we found it hard to invent sea.

Sometimes the land seemed
sweating with age,
and the wind swept large drops
on to the low plates of water
that were our dams and rivers.
On this coast, where we stand
on hills of marble crazed paving,
it is hard to invent land.

Like old people,
it grows small to survive,
much-walked-on island,
brothy with mist, whose shalebed,
shifting, left stone terrace everywhere,
nacreous, sea-few, tesserate,
shaping the mountain crest
to be a shade for water
under the webbing belt of heat,
the dead balance of sea.

II

The simplest things chill the heart:
the hare's elaborate haunches
belting the road
to Galway, running in the rising sun;

slow flash of woman
at the sea's edge: brown skirt,
maroon sweater: her hillside
slewbacked, buckled as gold,
and the hazels stiffened and silent
where in their flame-black
the mountain is setting.

From house to house grown-ups
live like spies, keeping
secrets in tin canisters.
Rain trails, thick as melting wax,
on their small tight windows.
The sun's final glitter falls
on the roof's shuddering antenna
and on the rooster, pearl-red,
shaking the spray from his neck.

III

The warm cloud dilates like an eye,
pulls invisibly at the seepings of grass.
Her hand on her face
pushing invisible strands
becomes solemn as a clock
as she wills herself
lifted up in her own sunset.

You'd fish all day for two lobsters.
The pots are filled with sea salt and seaweed.
The fish are dead, from the Atlantic
surge-line to the calmest southern harbour.
Windbent, in his crooked jersey
he stands above the ocean,
a hot brain fronting America,
and wills them back to his children.

The clarinet produced a clear colour
horizons could lower into it
and become sound, a line below the line of thinking,
pearl on pearl
a knifeblade in the white wineglass
fingers that search in the smoke for bites

          God gave you freewill,
          and you can use it for or against him,
          said the preacher.
          Like an old cowboy picture: God
          throws the gun between us,
          'Go for it when you're ready.'

You live in a world of small portions,
you eat from the cubist plate,
squares, oblongs, sharings of meat.
You can no longer contend for the hero's portion,
if you ever could, for it,
if it exists at all, is elsewhere.

Over and over again
the heart almost stopping
and the narrow heat in your mouth
as the tablet starts working.

It brings your memory back
Of your ride today in the tram
and the walk on the hot pavements
and the boys and girls straphanging

How quiet they are, the youth
of these days. Years ago
you rode in the same tram
and never stopped chattering

You criticised the German people
For not rising against Hitler
and blamed the Spaniards for Franco
and were just starting on Stalin

when the woman's voice attacked you.
There was always an adult voice
an authority shutting up schoolboys
warning you not to think.

Why do I think of that now,
in the evening, leaned back,
far from all those angers,
and widowed of brothers? Only

to see where my life has gone.
And it has gone, is thrown
as heavily as the gravel
over a million graves.

Dreamed

(What were they?) on one given moment,
one by one, each turned, going back
to their towns, places of origin,
homing. They raised their heads
at the lips of small mounds
with the pause in them, like salmon.
A stubbled field
lay there, a petrol station
breathed slackly over dull hedges.
Like animals, stunned with ancestral
fear, they sat wondering
foreheads pressed close to the twigs
still wet with ageing blossom
in the ruins of their beginning.

'All my life I hated afternoons,'
you seemed to have said in your letter.
I could understand that; it appealed to me
to hate time in sections,
like the withered outcrops of the jasmine,
they made the rest so pungent.

But you could hardly avoid them,
as we let them arrive
once a day, practising
their repertories of smiling
(of teacher, barber, doctor, playmate)
to settle us for the night.

You could have hated, simply,
the letters p.m., or the sun's
apricot glow, or the feeling
everything has been decided
and the day nowhere near ending

so that you'd spent it all too early

or digesting cut lunches.

I hated summers, and weekends,
when the noise came in like sunlight
that had already pushed in
like leaves, and branches, invoking other noises,
sounds of the paradeground of pleasure
when you rejoiced in unison,
swearing fealty to sand, sunscreen, Christmas,
and the idea of raging.
No-one was to be heard singing
alone, softly, in the dusk of evening.
You gave your assent to horns at midnight,
sirens at three a.m., the hoon bikes
revving in circles around the young girls
walking to the corner shop.
All was hedonism by agreement. In the summer,
that's when you feel unfree.

So many years ago, one year
when World War Two was coming clear,
Hess fell to earth near Glasgow town
and was captured by Jock Robertson.
All the Home Guard gathered round:
'I wouldn't shoot him on the ground.
The farmer there might overhear.
I would have shot him in the air.
But I'm sorry that he's had this strife,
locked up for so much of his life.
I would have shot him if I'd known.'
And entertained all Glasgow town.

Weird love, we coped together
like the two souls of a bad marriage
leaving, and bursting back,
and harping on each other
but more interested in talking promises
than keeping them.
And I've slept with you far too often
to have lost your smell or rhythm.

Cold love, many a time,
witch of the yellow mirror,
you had me up all night
to watch the lights, and next morning
like a spider from the ceiling
crawled inside my arms.

You tell me, now and again,
that the poets who praised whiskey
had raw, chafed skin; so that
by forty, they could not tell
one woman from another;
and how they were buying their gravestones
in the prime of their life.

Unfinished.

[160]

One put down his notebook
on the sand, among the shells,
and walked into the sea
whose foam seemed kinder than,
yes whiter than, blossom. Another
swam to a climax of drowning in his hometown river.
One cut her wrists, expecting
a great flow of wine. One tried to die of no sleep.
We did it without the American fad
of the loony-bin, with its frisson
and all the stories and anecdotes
it would lead to, and the portraits
of oldtimers, and the poems
polished like an apple to rough shine.
We let down in private, in secret;
suicide is not an export commodity
and will not come alive on air.
It is just the ending of this affair.

        It is like a work rhythm
        the sole tick tock that draws you,
        the to-fro of appetite,
        picking up, putting down,
        fishing in the fridge for a drink,
        eyes drowned with desire.
        You are listening for it now, the tick
        tock, the gluttony of loneliness
        that will eat your spirit
        as whiskey once did
        numb and eat.

        Madness will be your company,
        the dead who have come back
        to shine in the windows,
        the living indoors who
        will sit like shades in the chairs,
        their skin blown in by smiles.
        They are settled there, forever,
        stunned, in the glare of appetite.

Night-Walker

Who goes round my house all night,
with light and staring eyes?
None that Christian men could greet
except as prince of lies.

Who has life or time to sell
that old men might afford?
One that mocks and fares you well
with a hempen cord.

Who goes round, as on a rack,
flittering on tiptoe
as if the walls might crumble back
in dust like Jericho?

All the powers in me that fail
dressed in horns and hide
like a devil in a tale
who waits on the night tide.

Who walks and hums beneath his breath
this drear song or that?
One that has on loan from death
my whole habitat.

One who takes her final form
the midwife Furbelow
who grasped my hand when I was born
and would not let me go.

Series towards a longer
'BROUGHT UP ON THE FEARS OF WOMEN'

Civilisation has rebuked us all
with its barmy smile and suit clean as sherry.
It had not expected us to be so lonesome.
It aimed to take us all along
in its building programme. And there it is: it glitters
like the red-veined drawings in the *Home Medicine*,
its colours definite, primal, and exiguous,
so that the boy shuddered
every time he turned the pages to them.
It sets your memory running like a spool
to spin out, spin back, in sepia
those great divas of the artforms,
the fainting-spell, the midnight running
with arms akimbo flailing,
and nearer to our own day, the breakdown,
with its surreal and postmodern
choreography of suicide.

How porous it has all made us. Dinka,
after we took the razor from her,
cried; she had twisted her knee;
'I fell,' she kept saying, 'Why didn't
you stop me falling?' He had snapped the razor shut
and into his pocket. She would not let him help her up.
How abruptly the tears dry, how suddenly
the onlookers are weeping,
another getting ready for his turn.

Viewers are warned,
Some of these references may shock,
Some of these scenes you are about to witness
may startle the crab, clutch or bundle up
that breathlessness inside you

which jokingly you call the asthma-image
and its Munch-scream, or the blade
that spills the blood like soot
onto the panicky page of memory.

The Four Last Things:
Stench, fugue, blindness, the creeping in the body.

Male and female created he them,
Monsieur Couture. It was like blowing
a shelf of glass bubbles.
Male and female, the beautiful people
are strolling at length, in the *paseo*.
We have a saying, the debt collectors are out,
there are debts walking the boulevard,
each of these glances, every pause and gesture,
will have a rent to pay. Is that
a cynical saying? We have another:
We say, debt collectors
are expert at homemaking.

Only weeks from her death,
and smiling with the beautiful
fragile knuckles of her cheekbones,
she let the eyelids falter like steps
but still watched him,
touching the tips of his fingers: 'O Jack,
I'm sorry I mentioned him again.
I didn't mean to make you
unhappy.' Meaning jealous. Her amusement
at flirting and exasperating
an old lover. Who glowed with admiration.
Vital as sleep, it is this
that keeps her alive. This pressure keeps them,
skin and bone, deeply alive.
Saluting each other.
Yellow wildflowers in the grainy vase.

Dimly you could remember women's fears.
Automatically your hand swept your hair
against bats, last seen flashing and swooping
in the watery darkness of the lane.
Dark curved in and out of dark air.
High whistlers. Crazywings. Cave-bellies. Sickness.
Dogfaces. Stickers in webs. Deceivers. Harmless.
   Harmless.
When you are safely through their tunnel,
you will look back, triumphant as a baby.

Shrew. Shrew. What was it to be shrew?
Small face ambling into its corners
looking to bite at the wall-skirting.
The frenzied and desolate. Fount of nothing.
A hairy sinew scraping a shoe.
(By met.) a scolding woman.
(By extens.) a small boy
quiet as a circle, mouse-boy
delayed echo. A child could easily be lost here
among selves and pleasures.

The room, imagined
as a grassy bowl,
warm as if the sun
still burned around it,
could be your perfect setting,
interlocutors with touch, in form,
mother and son, your talk
lucrative with secrets.
An almost sulphurous depth of pleasure,
crisp curtain smells,
the Cassandra TV
clearing a space for your fears,
dread built into churchbells

and with unspoken pourings of blood
between you, like a contract,
and you are as close as any pair
of gossiping Cancerians,
badtempered and maternal.

Pregnant, or dying to be,
looking for every chance of a walk
on grass or leaves, to touch the skin of a tree,
to have a mad thirst for the black cherries,
but leave them urrpicked
(the crown of the boughs of their tribe),
to let the dog nose under your arm
yet brush down the breast where it dragged its muzzle,
these are a morning's fierce investings.
Not a stove in sight, not a man,
not a clutch of women. At most a book,
an inciting thump under the heart:
the game, sister, whose rules you carry.
You never thought so much, or talked so little,
as in those days.

The wand of light through on the table top
touches the silver band, moves eyes and hair
The arm she raised, not for the hand to open
but for strict relief, it is a wand too,
a rod of damaging, veined with white shadows.
Time flees from it, from every one of us,
in sharpened bits and edges. I end with no more
interest in myself
than in the moon

Years after you buried her
the spindle of her voice
swung round and round in the musicbox.
Waltz and polka flirted in it;
the frail machinery groaned
like damp ropes in the wind
to bring up a mother-figure, stepping,
wife, or sister, dancing before us
friends, daughters, whirling around us
all small puffed figures passing
into and out of
slits in the bright box,
whirling on fixed feet,
tipping fingers, kissing.
After the music, the important tears,
her breast and midriff held to yours
rich and curved as velvet.

Piece towards a longer
'BROUGHT UP ON THE FEARS OF WOMEN'

Brought up on the fears of women:
        all emissions of matter; intruders;
        fluxes of blood; marsh places;
        flooding and drought in the womb;
        the electricity of cats; stonefaced moons;
        HIM; uncensoring or mute gods;
        too close a brotherhood; and
        bats fertile as threads
        of excrement tugging the bedroots of the hair,
        getting into, into your brain;
        travel, unclean counterpanes . . .
Surrounded by this tenderness, he owned
his body like a patch of high ground.

        So learned about weakness;
        learned waiting;
        learned to outshift enemies;
        learned to traffic in mazes.

Eats with hands folded small, like paws.
Looks up, for a moment, sees the slitted wall
oozing some matter. Brushes at his hair

He has his old age already.
Scoured, electric.
Stands at the door-handle, attentive
the world floating like a retina

Whatever he rules, now,
it is by guile, flattery, dependence,
carefully timed punishment, divination.

Introduction for a Blues

We sat down four at the table
The coffee was silent and hot
The waitress was willing and able
But the conversation was not.

———

Two in a bed: cheap warmth
three in a bed: public transport

———

We made love on a daybed
clean as the telephone
the Japanese prints bedewed the wall
as coolly as your own

tapped on the cigarette box;
it's easy to make a home,
So long as you know who you're making it for;
it's easy to cry and come;

the poetry's left on the table
along with the unpaid bills,
we never learned to make coffee,
it's *cordon bleu* without frills.

While Bartok or Charlie Big Bird
spins carefully under glass
I leave you to make the daybed,
it's my weekday morning class.

There, where the committee voted, there's a proverb on
  the wall,
at this shining oval table, there's a message for us all,
an old message, about Newness, how it withers up and
  dies
unless we use old tricks to tease it, tricks of style, disasters,
  lies.

New reformers, new controllers, new men with their
  newest clones,
with their even newer women, and their future epigones,
turn the job-agreement over, turn you out of heart and
  home.
The new broom may sweep cleanest, but what will clean
  the broom?

>>>

I am leftwing going on rightwing,
steadfast as you can see
bank accounts guide me,
the best slogans hide me,
Factions were made for me.

O I am hardcore going on softcore
and soft is the hardest to be
Where shall I find a
useful reminder
if nobody contradicts me.

I am Recon. going on Decon
struction's the same for all
I'm leftwing rightwing
going on slowswing
over the garden wall

Money like lava
working unseen as pollen
shining like molten tin

worshipped on the clean phones
conjured up on the keyboard
communing in two kinds,
fax and thought transfer,

money like something in the food-chain,
steeped deep in the water-table
browning the edge of all the leaves,
killing weed and foetus,

spirit money. Money, wind and flame,
I'd rather bring back the old days
of greed and usury,
when we knew our enemy.

To write now is to breathe in death.
In twenty years they will call it context;
then, it will be background; then, climate.
We are living weather forecasts, not lives.

Young managers at the End of Century
are aesthetes, of course. In cool shirt sleeves
they move from room to room, talking tall,
and the manicured fax-sheets come to meet them.

The society was 'finely-realised',
like a poem. We could have stayed there,
adding to the complex balance, reading it
as if we were reading about ourselves.

I am stifling now because I breathed death.

I was no soldier. Buried here
I don't remember drill or drum
Loosed from savagery and fear,
I soften earth, until they come.

Two MPs marched me from my door
to force me into common weal
I trudged through eighteen months of war
and landed here

I was James Todd. My chain and watch
were all that vanished from this hole
in earth much like the scrawny patch
I farmed, one year, near Terrigal.

Bard-Price

This is the world as the hand of the killer displays it,
held up, shoved forward, with leaves of blood on the
   forehead,
Is this what the poet will celebrate, in the future court?
What he learned in darkness to compose in darkness

and sing with closed eyes? Food and drink are pressed on
   him,
women rub against him, he turns and jeers at servants.
Before he sings of victory, and of the severed heads,
it is a life of chiacking, learning the arts of mockery

if they're not to grow sick with dislike of one another.
He keeps the chanter in his bag, with the change of reeds
   and the cloths.
He carries his music inside him as they carry their
   massacres.

He was solitude by the river; he was the gaze-at-hunting
that fills the brain with harmonies, and gasps of new tunes.
He saw and drew up the images that wavered there, hour
   by hour,
as the eel slides, for mocking minutes, under the breast of
   the kingfisher.

Dialogues

Consciousness is irreversible, I said
In a hiss of sibilants,
Neglecting through my thinky joy
All the bleak evidence.

Writing about your own death
Is the trick no one can trump;
You have the joker in your hand
But there's this to remember,
You can only play him once.

      C. Wallace-Crabbe

Well, you may be right,
and your message timely.
In a life of sixty-three
years and a few months
it is no doubt something
to have played the Joker once.

It would be better to beat him,
mind you. Or do I mean her,
for I have a feeling that Jender
has run right through the pack
taken the King's curled beard
and cut the balls off Jack.

If you are so embarrassed,
shall I choose not to die,
nor to see the future
with carnal clarity?

True, each of us has in hand
one life, one world, one name.
But why are you insisting
there's only one game?

My instinct is to sing death-songs,
If they are well-musicked
they need disturb no-one
if I twist the ends of the tune
into further and further spirals
perhaps I can work them into jokes
out of this business of a man
setting out to sing death-songs.

Many chieftains have done this.
Sitting crouched near the ground
they rest the tips of their fingers
on the breath that lifts their ribs
and let the sun's heat fall
like a mantle on legs and shoulders.
Oh then the songs of the body.

But my friends rebuke me.
You should not have done it.
You must never try it twice

So I re-consider.
I take a guess about my forebears
and follow it right back
to the bits of bone and gristle
left on a ditch. Beginnings.

For A. D. Hope

I

Eyes everywhere, ready
to guide us into old age,
vestals, anxious lovers,
hurrying the past

back, reaching out to see
if something transparent
waits in the flesh, reserved,
rousing to shine at last.

This young one, detached
as her own hands, will feel
the man's profile as a courtesy
deepwhite as snow;

so that her eyes bring her back
to him, time and again,
like rain halting
at the edge of trees.

II

And they have watched you
more intently, the past years,
it may be an old friend
or love, chancing on you

at some conference, at dinner,
or a woman younger still
coming into your room
and sitting, staying on

with legs crossed, saying little,
or a girl student
with shy pawky face
straining to hear your

    soft rejoinders: their eyes touch you
    with cool fingers; their spirits
    bend, as if singing,
    bearers of death-linen.

For Brigid on Her Twentieth Birthday

We've had the magpies back again,
We've had the birthday shower of rain,
      The morning glinty,
And all the birds that know the song
Are pushing the quick tune along,
      Big Red's twenty.

We Irish have our very own
Goddess of love, and paragon,
      Name of Bridé.
The Bride's-day fires glow for her
Lustrous as her own red hair
      And twice as tidy.

Red they call her, Shining-clear . . .
A Pagan? It depends, my dear,
      On how you spell it.
She's like the sacred book itself,
Fresh-printed, yet not on the shelf,
      To hear *you* tell it.

Now blue patches thin the sky,
The garden's left to call and cry
      And streaming water,
The cats lie in the grass and peer
As if they might discover there
      An elder daughter.

Anyway, the birds don't care,
They slide and glitter in the air
      With songs of plenty
And need no urging, and no quarrel,
To sing as for a birthday carol,
      Red is twenty.

Birthday Poem for Grania

Whether or not we hear Thunder
As we ride in the clear air,
We can smell, here by the roadside,
The cut grass of the summer

Scented yellow. The swallows
Sew buttons on the air
And the calves rest low on their tails
That curve like braids of hair.

Susannah's Valentine

Was Valentine that pale captain
who stood nailed to a tree
with arrows in his coat-tails,
looking impossibly free?

Or was he the one with the hairdo
and the mustard-plaster face
with his limp hand stirring a book,
eyes on some old disgrace?

Or was he the running shepherd
whose sheep grazed close to the wall,
or the tumbler, the holy centurion,
the monk? Or, best of all,

was he the great entertainer
who sang you a song about wine?
He sends this verse; if you let him,
he'll be your valentine

Rudolph Valentino was sitting on the stair
Everyone pretended that he wasn't there
Rudolph Valentino come over here to me
And we'll dance around the Christmas tree.

Rudolph Valentino I don't care
Whether you are sitting on your stair
Rudolph Valentino come and play
And the Gwimsies can have an holiday.

Small Green Poem for Grania Buckley

Deer in the open grasses,
water seaming the rockface,
sunset red as bauxite,
thoughts quick as an eel-run.

The sound of your voice
the feet speeding like rain
the backward drift of your pale
hair flying: you are fanned by space.

You put the fringe of your hand
to my cheek; it is warm as a shawl
after the freeze of fog
that drew new shapes from the land.

For Susannah,
on returning from the Wards

Hospital was not for sleeping.
Who could sleep when, from all sides,
You had to hear the televisions shouting
New Romances, Jennifer and Matthew
at it in full colour:
'Our love is like a song,
We must tell the world.'
'No it must be a secret.'
'No it is like a song.'

On and on the disco-rock
Of love's debates, drilling through sick ears.

Now you have been released from
Your own Ward 101
(where sound, too, multiplies by 5)
home, with the neatest new scar
of all time under the gauze on your stomach,
you act out the whole scene,
you throw your head back like blows
of colour on a screen;
our love is like a good joke
the world may overhear.

―

You were walking
through the jets of music,
cornet, flute, oboe,
and she was crying
'I'm going to make Ireland.'
O I wish I could fly.
the sun-tiled, terraced mountains
built for a bugle's echo

He had tried to trust God.
Now he was crying out with his white stubble
and his hands mottled, 'Where wair you?'
'I waited here for yeh.
I did what you said.
Where did you get to? Where did you go?'
For God had demeaned him
with his squeeze of time.

But I don't know the way to Ireland.
The best bridges are of flesh and skin, Grania,
best blood is in hands touching
I cradle you low as an emerald
I'll write you gliding music,
crossing music, high bridge music.
Nostalgia can be the queen of the emotions.

Though I act out love and shake
With chills and fevers to my bones,
Nothing you do is for my sake;
Your smiles are merely overtones

To the heart's colour in your face.
But hope has made me desperate;
I follow you from place to place
Misreading signs, and daring fate.

Though I have been for twenty years
A victim of love's emphasis,
Though wounded in so many wars,
I fall to every trap there is:

I'm ambushed by your voice, your eyes'
Light misleads me everywhere,
I am dazed by your enterprise
And captured in your falling hair.

I aim, I know, at my own death,
Arranging the world to help us be
So loving that you draw my breath,
So intimate that you stifle me.

I try to reason but my heart,
That small unruly muscle, beats
Up blood against me, and I start
Forward into further nets.

So I pray my foolish prayer,
'Lord let me see her face again
Today, this minute; let this air
Light and me know her to the grain.'

Birthday Poem 2

Lucky the maker who receives
More than he understands:
A summer cool as autumn gives
Love into my hands.

Love, you make and heighten me
With every subtle breath,
A new earth and new man, set free
From the shape of his own death.

By mouth, eye, fingertip, and ear
My world of you is made
Body, while your loosened hair
Falls to the shoulderblade.

What brings the sweat into my eyes
And makes my skeleton
Tremble as though to recognize
Feeling and flesh are gone?

Why do I agonize to save
This hour of content
Whose dolphins bending through the wave
Hurry my banishment?

Still the sun in the rock-ledge
Pulses, and will not tire.
The soft lights at the ti-tree's edge
Flare like a summer fire.

Hill-Road

On that hill road the twisted
iron gate guarded the path
cool as an avenue.   Had
to balance on the planks, or
the straight nails tore your hands. Inside,
the abandoned farmer's kitchen,
the ancient feather mattress   full of dust
memory the pores of the skin

there we lay cool as dolphins
in the one wave   hearing

the cowman's distant voice a chain
unwinding, coming loose

hearing the possums
spatter and clutch like tree-strokes

on the iron roof.   And at last, at evening,
the sun in the green tree-level
flashed its wheel,
flashed, burning, going,
my hands under your shoulders

And years later   the evening's closed system
brings in the clear strained air
thunder rains, seeping
saffron through the grass paddocks

The air has no shadows
and the singing starts.   Froglight.
The evening opens in thunder

that pulls the sky down   flash on flash
gossiping and narrowing   lightning runs
around the house, downbeat at every window,
bringing through the copper wire
swathes of cool green, the animal
smell of dock, and straggling wet fern.

Burren

Our love that began with touching,
hair touching as it's blown,
and hands, and eyes, the too-much
wind-bitten feel of Miltown,

has been carried through fifty trials
yet stayed like a hare in its form.
The worries don't change, the wily
heart can't freshen its warmth;

on the straight road where he is running
the moon throws shivers of dawn.
The hare's run ends in the Burren,
and our love in Ballyvaughan.

I have you poised in the mind
Like an unbreaking wave

You, separate in your air,
Sitting always by the window,
Your colour changed, day by day,
But a flush leading down the cheekbones.
Your eyes dry, used to patience.

Seen always leaving rooms
With a small twist of the knee
As the door closes, and a linen
Freshness left across the air.

Water starts in my mouth
As if a spring there
Came from something spurting under my heart.
In the day, a great head of blossom.

That's how desire sets its mark,
Heartburn, water in the mouth
I move my knuckles down your thigh
Cold spaces enter the eye

Maladroit of words, ungoverned in body,
I'd rest you near my heart,
Your hands in the warmth of my shirt
an almost Alpine fragrance.

There is always a door to be gone out
Bare wood to be stared at
The small hinged window to be closed
Flat against the inrushing night.
Treading water on dry linoleum.

Sea-Mammal Songs

I

Kin-creatures. They came like
breasts of horses in the sea;
figments of Dionysos,
lent their backs to Arion,
who sang from the deck, high, high,
whose harp lights and hisses
in the water: calling
'Simo. Simo', a name that brings
their dark backs to the shore.

Eyes wide as a horse's
flukes steady as hands
holding up their dead,
the high shoulder weeping,
lent their voice to Arion,
held noon rites in the shallows,
took fish from a spear-tip,
and came gently to the Dreamer,
the porpoise-caller, who would still
not speak their names in his dreaming.

II

At Lorne pier, in broad daylight,
the jaw-shaped mussels clacked
like bats under roof-joists,
and the redfaced fishermen,
weathered sea-husbandmen,
stood on the edge, their rifles
picking the dolphins off.

Years later, one winter Sunday,
as we walked on Lorne pier,
and the unarmed fishermen
talked, halting, to each other,
the fish smelt urinous,
the air dark as creosote
flickered and faded
where their gunsmoke had hung
on Erskine's still, heavy mouth.

III

You were the heat of the sea,
the coast's electric echo,
bodies warming bodies,
skin after skin rubbed off
on every flank of earth,
that great wet rolling back
that surfaced like a heart
or hung in weak sleep
became our soul's horizon.

IV

My dead mother, who left me
the lizard pouch on the eye
and my mind scuttling
like a crab's mouth,
surely you could have taught me
to distinguish
the dolphin's whistle: in the rush of trees,
or bursting asphalt, my own
eternity flexing around me;
and the Celts, with their sea-flukes
and new gills, travelling

V

following the spoor of the sea
into your words, the sonar
pulse of memory,
silk tissue of fingertip,
you saw, not heard, their urging
whistle; so your poem
may hold up a few dead,
your whistling sigh of love
help a hard few to breathe.

Sit on the counter, girl, and dress your hair
with a bounce of your head for every ringing year;
the music swells from every shelf behind you
and a blue clock striking into its note reminds you

here's morning: Too new for most of us,
who are still caught in the steam, or oil, or rust,
of the travelling life, crossing some railway line.
On the timber fence the passionflower vine

straightens up, into the sun, that swivels low.
The imagination lazing from blow to blow
of sparkling fact, will come as soon as it can
to find you fully dressed, with watering-can.

Parson Dadewell with his curates,
Squire with his retinue,
histories of the chidden people
lost, forever, to the view,
all of these come up in music
to utter their lost lives anew.

Doctor calls his flirting widow,
Farmer Gauger late at plough
lies in Briston churchyard grunting
as he ploughs Miss Kitchen now,
arses open to the weather
like the hedges, row on row.

Late spring is the time for pleasure,
the sun climbs up the moon at swell,
and lives engaged with this bold advent
all rouse up their parable,
all arise and cry their message:
Death hólds us, and hólds life as well.

I wrote a letter to Seamus
but Seamus never replied.
I think it's possible Seamus is Irish.
'O he is! He is!' They cried.

I wrote a letter to Seamus
and Seamus said not a word.
It's better to write on a Saturday night
and send it by way of a bird.

I wrote a letter to Seamus
and Seamus sent back a note;
'A chara, I'm sorry, I didn't
get any of the letters you wrote.'

I wrote a letter to Seamus,
Seamus was having a drink.
He said, 'Oh dear! We can't have him here!
What will the neighbours think?'

I sent a letter to Seamus
And what did Seamus say?
He said, 'In each season, for whatever reason,
I'm going to be away.'

Child of Ardmore

There's fish on the rooftop and ink in the sea
And the larks on the headland are whistling at me
I'll run by the woodland and look for a hare
And deep in the paddock the tractor is there

> *The cliffs of Ardmore*
> *The mists of Ardmore*
> *And the children at play on the strand,*
> *The roads to the tower*
> *The soft booming hour*
> *Of the sea that runs under the land.*

There's eels in the coalbox and carrots in grass
And the teddy bears watch from their seats under glass
I'll hunt to Goat Island and fish out the sun
That colours the red marble veins of the stone

> *Refrain*

Down in the Main Street there's plenty to see
But more when there's only my Grandmam and me
A wave hisses over and jumps on her back
And I'm left, as so often, to carry her pack

> *Refrain*

St Declan came here in the dawn of the years
And built with his fingers the place without tears
There the pines in the wind blossom up like a kite
And at evening you'll see the small prows of the light

> *Refrain*

Ardmore Bay

This morning in the tiding the waves were green with
    spray
And the land seemed moving outward from the sea.
Though I must leave it soon, to go twelve thousand miles
    away,
Ardmore will never see the last of me.

> *The angles of the light*
> *And the blackbirds in their coursing*
> *They fall away together*
> *To the wide strand of Ardmore.*

The people in their kindness, in the delicate deep town,
They're living out the dignity of Here:
The sea they'll walk in summer, the land they'll keep their
    own,
This is the Ireland no-one has to fear.

> *O the angles of the light*
> *And the small birds in their coursing*
> *They lift away together*
> *From the headlands of Ardmore.*

The seagulls come down grunting on the tailspin of the
    gale,
They are speaking Munster Irish to our heart;
The past that gives us courage will keep our country whole
And the future lift away the bitter part.

> *The angles of the light*
> *And the blackbirds in their coursing*
> *They fall away together*
> *To the wide strand of Ardmore.*

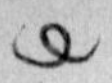